Supporting Maths & English in Post-14 Education & Training

Supporting Maths & English in Post-14 Education & Training

Jo-Ann Delaney and Amanda Cope

 Open University Press

Open University Press
McGraw-Hill Education
8th Floor
338 Euston Road
London
NW1 3BH

email: enquiries@openup.co.uk
world wide web: www.openup.co.uk

and Two Penn Plaza, New York, NY 10121-2289, USA

First published 2016

A catalogue record of this book is available from the British Library

ISBN-13: 978-0-33-526410-0
ISBN-10: 0-33-526410-7
eISBN: 978-0-33-526411-7

Library of Congress Cataloging-in-Publication Data
CIP data applied for

Typeset by Aptara, Inc.

Printed and bound by CPI Group (UK) Ltd, Croydon, CR0 4YY

Praise for this book

"For teachers faced with the blithe demand to embed English and Maths in their teaching of other subjects, Delaney and Cope offer help in the shape of this well-informed, clearly constructed and very readable book. These experts in English and Maths have ensured that their advice is well conceived and carefully explained but also that it is practical. Written with enthusiasm and flair, this book is valuable and very welcome."

Professor Kevin Orr, School of Education and Professional Development,
University of Huddersfield, UK

"This book is a very welcome resource to help further, adult and vocational teachers in supporting their learners' English and maths skills as part of their subject learning. It is clearly-written and practical, providing help in motivating students and activities that can be adapted to embed English and maths learning in other subjects. The book should be widely used by individual teachers in any subject area, and also as a key text for teacher education."

Jay Derrick, Director of Teacher Education (post-compulsory),
University College London Institute of Education, UK

"Supporting English and Maths in Post-14 Education and Training is a practical guide for vocational and specialist teachers who are non-specialists in English or Maths. The book provides accessible and practical ways of embedding aspects of English and Maths (literacy and numeracy) into our own teaching. From reading aloud to pronunciation on the one hand; and from measurement and data handling on the other, the authors present workable strategies, ideas and exercises that are easy to use. Jargon-free and user-friendly, this book offers valuable insights and ideas."

Dr Rebecca Eliahoo, Principal Lecturer (Lifelong Learning),
University of Westminster, UK

Contents

Acknowledgements

We would like to thank our colleagues in the Post-Compulsory Education and Training Phase at Canterbury Christ Church University, who supported us in the writing of this book, providing encouragement, feedback and chocolate.

Special thanks go to Phil Cope for his help with some of the maths diagrams and the many cups of tea.

We would also like to thank all our trainee teachers, who continue to inspire us.

Preface

The idea for this book arose out of our experience working with trainee teachers on our teaching education programmes at Canterbury Christ Church University. Faced with demands to 'embed English and maths' in their teaching, trainees struggled with the concept and sometimes with their own personal skills in English and maths. They also became disillusioned with what seemed to them being asked to teach subjects outside their own area in which they felt they lacked expertise.

We have tried to write this book as a practical solution to the issues our trainee teachers face, but also for practising teachers who may also find the emphasis on English and maths across the curriculum somewhat of a challenge. We have not set out to write an English or maths textbook, but in order to support teaching activities, we have included opportunities for teachers to check their own understanding and skills.

In each chapter, a range of vocational areas is used to provide examples of activities for embedding. It will be up to each teacher to adapt and apply the examples to their own subject. We hope that you will gain a lot of teaching ideas as well as more general principles about how English and maths can be developed.

The book is aimed very much at non-specialists of English and maths rather than teachers of these subjects. The explanations are accessible and there is recommended follow-up reading should you decide you wish to develop your skills further.

We hope that the book will provide you with practical classroom strategies for enjoying work with English and maths within your subject specialism.

1 English and maths across the curriculum

Introduction

The title of this book only names the subjects of English and maths, but in some ways this book is less about English and maths and more about other subjects taught in the curriculum of the further education and skills sector. The book reflects on where English and maths can be found within other subjects and suggests how teachers of other subjects might begin to use opportunities to develop their learners' English and maths skills.

It could be argued that it is equally important to write about the place of science, history or geography in other subjects. Indeed, many schools and colleges have developed cross-curricula strategies that acknowledge that individual subjects, each of which represents a particular area of knowledge, don't exist in isolation.

Why, then, is there such a focus on English and maths in the further education and skills sector? English or language is, of course, the key to communication, both written and spoken. We would not be able to function very effectively as human beings if we were unable to communicate – it is part of what makes us human. Maths is equally important in providing us with the key to understanding the way our universe functions. However, also at play are a number of educational, political and social factors that have contributed to the current interest in – some might say hysteria about – English and maths.

English and maths at the core of the curriculum

1999 – The 'Moser Report'

A good place to start with an exploration of the reasons why we are concerned with English and maths is a government report entitled 'A Fresh Start', but more often referred to as the Moser Report after the chair of the committee that undertook the research, Sir Claus Moser. The committee investigated the standards of English and maths, referred to as *Literacy* and *Numeracy*, in England. It came up with some quite startling findings. Examples included:

- Some 7 million adults in England – one in five adults – when given the alphabetical index to the *Yellow Pages*, cannot locate the page reference for plumbers. That is an example of functional illiteracy. It means that one in five adults are less literate than would be expected of an 11-year-old.
- Something like one in five adults have very low numeracy: one in three adults in England cannot calculate the area of a room measuring 21 × 14 feet, even with the aid of a calculator.

While both the methods for collecting the data and the generalizability of the findings in the report have been called into question, there is no doubt that the headline-grabbing '7 million adults in England are illiterate' was inevitably going to influence government policy.

The consequent 'Skills for Life Initiative' launched in 2001 aimed to tackle the low levels of literacy and numeracy. Large amounts of funding were provided to make literacy and numeracy classes more readily available, with more teaching hours. New core curricula for literacy, numeracy and ESOL (English for Speakers of Other Languages) were introduced. Qualifications for teachers of those subjects were revised to include a greater emphasis on subject knowledge and subject-specific pedagogy. Qualifications for learners were also revised and the existing 'Key Skills' qualifications were supplemented by 'Skills for Life' qualifications in literacy, numeracy and ESOL from Entry to Level 2 (GCSE equivalent). To acknowledge the different needs of Entry-level learners, three sub-levels (Entry 1, Entry 2 and Entry 3) were introduced.

The advent of functional skills

In 2008, a suite of vocationally oriented 'New Diplomas' was introduced. Although these qualifications were never fully established by the time a new government was in power, they did include new qualifications for English and maths: Functional Skills. These were to replace the old Skills for Life qualifications for literacy and numeracy; ESOL remained outside the Functional Skills framework.

These new qualifications were designed to contextualize work with English and maths so that learners could see the relevance of these subjects to real life. This was meant to allow teachers to provide contexts for English and maths work in their lessons that were linked directly to the other subjects they were studying.

From Leitch to Wolf

Subsequent government reports continued to highlight the need for developing the English and maths skills of all learners. The Leitch review of skills (2006) placed a renewed emphasis on the need for English and maths to be at the core for the creation of 'world-class skills' that would enable Britain to become more competitive in the industrial world. Employers were given an increased voice in the discussion, highlighting how poor standards of English and maths were hampering their ability to provide jobs for learners leaving colleges with good vocational qualifications.

The Wolf review of vocational education (2011) continued the focus on English and maths as core to any vocational curriculum. Under a new government, this report resulted in a higher profile being given to the GCSE qualification and a grade 'C' at GCSE becoming a new benchmark for success instead of the existing Functional Skills qualifications. This shift in priority signalled a revised focus on a more academic version of English and maths reflected in the dropping of *literacy* and *numeracy* in the titles of qualifications for teachers of the subjects.

GCSE

The emphasis placed in the Wolf review on attaining an A*–C grade in GCSE continues to impact teachers of all subjects working in the further education and skills sector. The attainment of the GCSE grade has become a benchmark of success for learners, which means that all programmes have to ensure that learners who start a new programme without a GCSE in English and maths have to continue their studies in those subjects. From September 2014, this requirement became a condition of funding for programmes.

The question arises whether the more academic GCSE qualification is attainable or desirable for all learners. It is possible for learners to study other qualifications such as Functional Skills where a GCSE A*–C is not immediately attainable, but these are seen as 'interim' or 'stepping-stone' qualifications on the journey towards achieving a GCSE.

What about teachers of other subjects?

Up to now, we have looked at policies and reports that have had a huge impact on English and maths teachers and learners. Parallel to all these developments was a growing expectation that all teachers in the further education and skills sector would become quasi teachers of English and maths. A key development was the revision of teaching qualifications for all teachers in the sector in 2007. Introduced with the aim of professionalizing the workforce and moving towards parity with secondary school teachers, the revision made clear that all teachers were expected to use opportunities in their subject lessons to address the English and maths (and ICT) skills of their learners. In order to facilitate this, a 'Minimum Core' of knowledge was to be introduced into all teaching qualifications.

The Minimum Core

The Minimum Core covered two aspects. The first was teachers' own personal skills in English and maths, which were expected to be at least Level 2. There was, and currently is, no requirement for teachers in the sector to have a qualification in English and maths prior to entry onto a teaching qualification, unlike primary and secondary teachers. The introduction of the Minimum Core was seen as an attempt to encourage teachers to embrace opportunities to further develop their own skills in these two subjects.

The second aspect covered by the Minimum Core was a knowledge and understanding of how English and maths skills are developed. It included an understanding of why learners may not have the skills required and how to use opportunities to develop those skills within the subject lessons.

The 2014 'Professional Standards for Teachers and Trainers in Education and Training – England' have continued the emphasis on teachers of other subjects embedding English and maths. As part of their *Professional Skills* (standard 16), teachers should:

> Address the mathematics and English needs of learners and work creatively to overcome individual barriers to learning.

Embedding

Along with the Minimum Core, colleges and other organizations within the sector were being encouraged to *embed* English and maths in different ways across the curriculum. At an organizational level, there are different models for embedding and the models described below are broadly those that have been implemented with different degrees of success in different organizations. In many places, one model was trialled only to be replaced by another. The models are now described as well as some of the advantages and limitations of each.

Model 1: Discrete provision
In this model, the learners attend separate English and maths lessons in groups usually organized according to level, such as groups of Level 1 maths

learners from different subject areas studying in a class together. It is likely that a renewed focus on GCSE English and maths will encourage this model to be used more widely, as the GCSE curriculum lends itself to discrete delivery and specialist teachers are normally used.

Advantages

- Learners work at the same level and resources can be tailored for the specific level.
- Lessons are usually taught by subject specialists, who have a good knowledge of subject pedagogy.

Limitations

- English and maths are decontextualized from the vocational area learners are studying. This is likely to be demotivating and to lead to learners questioning the value of English and maths, which they see as being separate from what they really want to learn.

Model 2: Subject teacher teaches English and maths
In this model, the subject teacher delivers English and maths in a way that they are fully integrated within the subject timetable. Learners stay in the same group and there is a perceived seamlessness between the vocational subject and English and maths classes.

Advantages

- Learners can see the relevance of English and maths more clearly, as links are continuously made with their chosen subject.
- The teacher can contextualize all the English and maths work, as they are expert in the vocational subject.

Limitations

- The teacher may lack confidence in their own personal skills in English or maths and this may prevent them from preparing effective learning activities.
- Learners are likely to have different levels of English and maths and, by staying in one group, their needs might not be met.

Model 3: The collaborative approach
In this model, the English and maths specialist teachers work with the vocational teacher. Ideally, they plan the programme together to ensure that all English and maths lessons are contextualized in the vocational subject. This might involve the English and maths teachers sitting in on the vocational lessons to gain awareness as to what they should focus on in their lessons.

Advantages

- The English and maths lessons can be fully contextualized, making the content relevant to learners and providing a more joined-up curriculum.

Limitations

- This is potentially the most costly approach, as time needs to be allocated to both the subject and English/maths specialist to develop their specific lessons and to collaborate on the planning of the curriculum.
- It is a staffing-intensive model. It is likely that each curriculum area needs its own English/maths specialist, who can become more expert in the vocational subject.

It is likely that Model 3 would be the most effective, but also the least likely to be fully implemented because of the costs involved.

Embedding for the teacher of other subjects

Teachers' standards, the aims of your organization, and the general requirements of teachers in the sector, all place a clear emphasis on the role of the teacher in developing their learners' English and maths skills. It is likely that you need to demonstrate that you are doing this in your schemes of work, lesson plans and resources.

Teachers face some challenges in implementing the embedding agenda. The first of these is confidence in one's own personal skills in English or maths. For English, it may be that you feel confident in your everyday use of language, but do not feel able to explain features of the language to your learners. For maths, the lack of confidence is often more profound, with teachers hesitating to explore even quite common mathematical functions with their learners though a lack of confidence on their own part.

Many organizations offer additional professional development opportunities to both enhance teachers' personal skills and offer them strategies for embedding English and maths in their lessons. There are also numerous resources available with ideas for working with English and maths within your subject area.

The aims of this book in relation to embedding

This book is intended to provide insight into some of the principles of embedding English and maths. It has ideas for classroom activities, but also suggests some general approaches that you can adapt to your own subject area, specific lessons and groups of learners you are teaching.

The purpose of this book is, therefore, to provide a resource on *how* to address English and maths in the teaching of your subject area. The structure of each chapter follows a similar pattern to cover both the enhancement of your own English and maths awareness as well as giving you ideas for embedding.

The first aim of each chapter is to provide some background knowledge in relation to a particular aspect of English or maths. This section is deliberately written for non-specialists and should hopefully offer an insight into some key concepts in an accessible manner. If you would like to learn more about a particular aspect of English and maths, additional resources are suggested at the end of each chapter.

The second aim is to provide you with ideas for classroom activities to develop English and maths skills. In order to illustrate each idea, we provide examples related to a specific subject area. It would be impossible to provide an example for every curriculum area of the further education and skills sector; instead, the principles behind the idea are discussed so that you can apply them easily to your own subject.

We have used the term 'embedding' throughout this book because it is both familiar and commonly used within the sector. It is important at this stage to consider what embedding actually means and what it might look like in your own lessons.

Identifying opportunities

Often in schemes of work, opportunities for working with English or maths are identified. For example, a lesson might include an activity that involves the taking of notes, which is a writing and listening skill, or looking at the word count for assignments, which is a numerical skill. There is a clear difference, however, between identifying these opportunities and using them to develop English and maths. This difference is illustrated in Table 1.1.

For some teachers, the challenge arises when they are asked to use an existing scheme of work with opportunities for English and maths development clearly identified, but may have no idea as to how these areas might be addressed. It general, it is ideas for practical classroom activities that are elusive. Hopefully, this book will help in such circumstances.

Table 1.1 Identifying opportunities vs. developing skills

Teacher identifies opportunities	Teacher develops skills
English	
Learners take notes	• Learners work in groups to discuss how to take notes effectively
	• Learners practise with a short mini-lecture
	• Learners compare 'notes' and develop a list of good practice tips for note-taking
Maths	
Learners produce word count of assignments	• Learners discuss how to estimate calculation
	• Learners try out estimation strategies using addition and multiplication and check with computer calculation
	• Learners discuss benefits of estimation and other contexts where it can be used

Contextualization

Another term that is used to describe the inclusion of English and maths across the curriculum is *contextualization*. This means providing a real context for the English and maths content within the subject area being taught. This is something that might be done by the teacher of the vocational subject but also by an English or maths teacher, who would aim to provide an engaging situational exploration of an English or maths topic.

Suggestions on how to use this book

Each chapter contains many ideas for your teaching but also useful background knowledge to enhance your awareness of English and maths. We suggest you consider the two elements alongside each other, as a greater awareness is likely to give you the confidence and skills to address English and maths in your own subject area. This is not intended as an English or maths textbook, although there are references to further reading if you wish to deepen your knowledge. However, one of the premises of the book is that English and maths are interesting, relevant and important and worth finding out more about! We hope the book will inspire you to inspire your learners.

Part 1
Supporting English in Post-14 Education and Training

2 Introduction to English

Reflective task – quiz about English

Try answering the following questions about English. You will find the answers at the end of the chapter.

1. How many people in the world speak English?
2. Which of the following languages have contributed words to English: French, Norse, German, Czech, Gaelic?
3. How many different sounds are there in English?
4. What percentage of the world's electronic information is stored in English?

Introduction

It would be helpful for you and your learners to know some general facts about English, such as the ones referred to in the quiz above. Having some background as to the origins of the language and current issues also provides a context for some of the areas dealt with in later chapters.

In this chapter, we look at the development and spread of English in an attempt to understand some of the issues that are discussed later. We also describe the structure of the English sections of the book and explain why the content on English is divided the way it is.

History of English

A consideration of the emergence and continued development of the English language provides a useful starting point for explaining some of the different aspects of English that can be both challenging and interesting for your learners. This is a very brief overview.

The origins of English lie in the numerous invasions by other nations of the land mass we now call Great Britain. The invaders conquered the indigenous tribes, imposing their language upon them. The invaders were mainly from Germanic tribes: the Angels from the area that is now Denmark, the Saxons from what we now call Germany, and the Frisians from the area that is now the Netherlands in the fifth and sixth centuries. English is therefore a Germanic language and some of its structures and words are related to modern German. This new, imposed language replaced the original Celtic languages, which were driven back to the more outlying regions of Great Britain – Scotland, Wales and Cornwall.

Throughout history, there have been many other influences, including major contributions from French. The English language has therefore developed a tolerance to the influence of other languages and has changed accordingly – this has been a major strength in terms of its survival as the native language of Great Britain.

Another result of this absorption of other languages is that there are many irregularities in grammar and spelling. Since English words and sentence structures have their origins in several different languages, it is to be expected that they will be subject to different rules. It can be frustrating for learners to find that, when looking for rules, there are so many exceptions. When asked why a word or a sentence is constructed the way it is, the only answer sometimes is that is the way it has evolved! A logical explanation of some of the rules is often not possible.

The spread of English

Due mainly to the growth of the British Empire, English has spread throughout the world and is the first or second language of many nations. The spread has been bolstered in the last two centuries by the emergence of the United States as a global military and economic power.

A further reason for the spread of English is its use in computing and on the internet. That so much electronic data is currently stored in English guarantees its place as the first language of the internet and social media.

The fact that English is widely spoken and understood can be an advantage for learners whose area of study will lead them to a profession that involves international work, such as business studies or leisure and tourism. There is also the disadvantage, however, that being an international language, speakers of English may be discouraged from studying other languages and therefore other cultural contexts. It can reinforce the idea that if you speak English, it is not necessary to learn another language.

Embedding ideas

It is important that learners both understand the importance of English as an international language and appreciate the value of learning another language(s). Below we offer some ideas for you to use in the classroom.

Embedding ideas

✔ Encourage learners to research topics such as those highlighted in the quiz at the beginning of the chapter. This could be in relation to their chosen area of study, such as subject-related words that they will need to learn. For example, learners in catering might find it interesting to investigate the French terms they use.

✔ If there are learners in the group who speak other languages, encourage them to teach the rest of the class common phrases, such as how to greet one another. Learning how to spell and say first names can also be a way to explore how other languages work and how they sound.

Language change

A language must change over time if it is to be a living language. As Latin is no longer spoken and therefore cannot change, it is not a living language. English, on the other hand, is a living language and is constantly changing. Its ability to absorb and accommodate new language rules and items allows it to be flexible and nimble as regards new words and structures.

The capacity for language to change allows it to alter over time and also to be altered when used in different places. As highlighted above, English is used in many different countries of the world and as a means of electronic communication. It should be of no surprise, then, that there are many different *varieties* of English or ways of using English that are particular to a group or groups of people who interact with one another in English.

It is not clear whether the flexibility of English has contributed to its spread throughout the globe or whether its spread has forced upon it an element of flexibility. For some people, however, such flexibility is a cause for concern and there is a view that we should be searching for a standard language that is less susceptible to change. Some people argue that we should have very fixed rules about how English is spoken and written, and that any divergence from these rules should be considered *incorrect* usage. Different groups and individuals hold different views on this issue, and we explore these both here and in later chapters.

Language variety

The changes that began to occur as English spread to other countries led to the development of different language varieties. A variety is a type of English that is spoken by a group of people distinct from another group. To illustrate what makes up a variety, let us consider two of the varieties of English that are geographically based: British English and General American. Examples of the differences are illustrated in Table 2.1. These encompass the way the language is spoken as well as some features of writing. In general, it is the features of spoken language that are most noticeably different, as written language tends to change little.

Table 2.1 Differences between British English and General American

Difference in:	British English	General American
Pronunciation	**Door** ('r' not pronounced) **Student** ('y' sound before the 'u')	**Door** ('r' pronounced) **Student** (no 'y' sound)
Words	Lift Puncture Block of flats	Elevator Flat tyre Condominium
Grammar	I've done that already If I had known, I'd have told you	I did that already If I would have known, I'd have told you

The example in Table 2.1 is of a geographical or regional variety, where the location of the English speaker determines the variety. There are, of course, other determinants of variety, such as age. People of a different generation, even within the same family, may use different words to describe the same thing.

As a general rule, the differences between varieties do not cause many misunderstandings. Spoken communication is usually helped by facial expression and an ability to ask for clarification. Written communication tends to use a more standard language and there is no accent or pronunciation involved. What can be an issue, however, is the positive or negative value placed on a variety and the continued discussion around the notion of a *Standard English*.

Standard English

It is important to have rules about the way a language is used to avoid confusion in communication and to prevent it becoming gibberish. There are rules of use in English, which we learn as we learn the language, but we tend not to be conscious of them. Breaking these rules can lead to a breakdown in communication, but rarely to the extent that speakers cannot understand one another.

The search for a standard form of English can, however, lead to an attitudinal stance whereby a variety that is considered non-standard is seen as having less value. This can sometimes be seen in the way regional accents are ridiculed. The impact can be quite serious, with individuals being denied opportunities or judged as less intelligent or less able because of their language variety, mostly in relation to their spoken language. This issue is discussed in more detail in Chapter 6.

The value placed on a standardized form of written English will play a role in many of the situations your learners will find themselves in. These include writing essays or course work, applying for jobs of entrance to university, as well as a range of formal communication tasks. It is important that you encourage learners to use Standard English and an appropriate level of formality in these contexts. They are unlikely to get a job if their application is written in text speak, for example.

The chapters in this book on English take the view that you should be guiding your learners to use Standard English, but that the flexible nature of English lends itself to more interesting work in the classroom. By recognizing non-standard forms, you can introduce both a fun element to the lesson and develop your learners' awareness of the different varieties. Consider the following sets of classroom activities and decide which might be more engaging for your learners.

Lesson activity 1

Either: Write a paragraph arguing against action on global warming.
Or: Look at the paragraph arguing against action on global warming, it is written in text speak. Rewrite it in formal English.

Lesson activity 2

Either: Summarize the key message from the text.
Or: Write a tweet (140 characters) to encapsulate the key message from the text.

It is likely that the alternative activity suggested will prove more engaging for learners and will raise their awareness of both standard and non-standard written English. How appropriate each activity would be may depend on the subject or the level the learners are working at.

Organization of chapters on English

Four chapters look at embedding English. They are organized around different aspects of English and represent the different language areas that might provide opportunities for developing the English skills of your learners.

The 'four skills'

Three of the four chapters consider the four skills of language: reading, writing, speaking and listening. This is a convenient way to organize the content, as it corresponds well with the types of activities that you might use as part of your subject lessons. Hopefully, it will also allow you to identify opportunities for embedding more easily. For example, if your lesson includes an activity in which learners read a text, you can consult the chapter on 'Reading'.

When considering the four skills, it is useful to look at reading and listening together. This is because reading and listening skills involve the receiving of language input and are often called *receptive* skills. It follows that similar activity types would be useful for developing both reading and listening. It is also useful to think of a *text* as something that can be written *or* spoken. Therefore, the ideas that can be used to help learners access written texts can equally be used to support them in work with spoken texts.

Writing and speaking are considered together for the same reasons as outlined above in relation to reading and listening. In both writing and speaking, language is produced and so these skills are often called *productive* skills. However, it is recognized that some of the complexities of speaking are unique to this skill, particularly for learners who do not have English as their first language. Therefore, there is an additional chapter on speaking in general and with a specific focus on learners for whom English is an additional language.

Pronunciation and speaking

Another skills chapter considers the area of speaking in more detail and focuses in particular on issues around pronunciation. There is a section on general awareness activities for all learners, but there is a more detailed consideration of how you can support learners who do not have English as their first language.

The 'four skills' focus should hopefully allow you to identify easily the opportunities in your subject area for embedding the development of English language skills. The activities and ideas suggested provide a framework for matching your embedding activities to those that occur naturally as part of the subject content of the lesson.

Words and sentences

The remaining chapter in the English section considers work that you might do on words and sentences, often called grammar and vocabulary. In this chapter, some of the common grammatical areas are looked at and there are ideas for including a focus on words and sentences in your teaching and also in the way you correct learners' work. To an extent, this chapter revisits the areas addressed in writing and speaking.

For some teachers, the thought of dealing with something related to grammar can be quite off-putting. Every attempt has been made to ensure the content of this chapter is accessible to everyone and there is further recommended reading if you are interested in looking at this area in more detail.

English not as a first language

It is important at this stage to clarify the terms we use in relation to learners for whom English is not a first language. As outlined at the beginning of this book, there are many people who speak English as a second (or third or fourth) language rather than as their first language. Their capacity for using English may be identical to or similar to those who learned English as a first language, often called native speakers. Others may have English language skills considerably less developed than native speakers. A range of terms is used in the educational field to describe these learners, as highlighted below. Different people may use the terms slightly differently, so the explanations given below are quite generalized.

ESOL

ESOL, or *English to Speakers of Other Languages,* is the name given to the subject of English when taught to people who do not speak English as their first language. However, it has come to be used as a describing word for those learners: 'ESOL learners'. It is commonly used like this in the further education context and is well known and understood by teachers of other subjects. For this reason, it is used in this book as well as the description: 'learners whose first language is not English'.

The term ESOL recognizes the fact that these learners are actually very language proficient and can speak other another language or languages. The term tries to acknowledge the capacity of these learners rather than their limitations with English. The term also suggests that as teachers of these learners, we should remain aware of their considerable linguistic skills of working with more than one language, rather than focusing solely on the errors they might make when using English.

ESL

The term ESL, *English as a Second Language,* suggests that the learner has one other language and is learning English to enhance their language skills. It is a term most commonly used in education systems in North America.

EAL

Again the term EAL, *English as an Additional Language,* refers to the capacity of the learner to speak other languages and that speaking English will add to the skills they already possess. This term is more commonly used with younger learners in primary and secondary schools in the UK when improving their English skills alongside the other curriculum subjects.

EFL

EFL, *English as a Foreign Language,* is a term used to describe learners who wish to study English as a language for leisure or business. It suggests a more temporary learning activity, such as enrolling in an evening course in their home country to become more language proficient or studying for a short period of time in an English-speaking country to develop specific language skills to use in work or leisure.

Bilingual learner

Although the term 'bilingual' is more often used to describe someone who is equally proficient in two languages, the term can also be used to acknowledge the capacity and skills of those simply living and working with more than one language. It can be a very positive term, focusing on the possession of skills rather than their absence.

The structure of the chapters on English

Each chapter starts with **a reflective task** designed to get you thinking about the content of the chapter, as was the case at the beginning of this chapter. The reflection activity is designed for you, but could equally be used with your learners. Once you have completed the reflection activity, you will find a suggested answer or commentary at the end of the chapter. In some chapters, the answers to the reflection activities are linked to the sections of the chapter content.

The first part of the chapter provides information about English to make you more aware of different aspects that will help you to support your learners. The content is accessible and provides an introductory understanding of each aspect. Further reading is provided at the end of each chapter should you wish to gain a deeper understanding of any topic.

The rest of the chapter is devoted to ideas and activities that you can use in the classroom to develop your learners' English skills. Many of the ideas are contextualized in a specific subject area, but provide general principles of how to construct the teaching and learning activity in your own subject area. The main formats are:

- **A description** of an activity that can be used in a lesson to embed English. It is up to you to adapt this to your subject area.
- **An example** of an activity from a specific subject area, such as a writing task from a Leisure and Tourism lesson. Key features of the activity are highlighted so that you can design a similar activity in your own subject area.
- **Some general advice** or 'dos and don'ts' about an aspect of embedding English. These might be general tips or hints about how to approach a particular area or perhaps a warning about things to avoid.
- **A commentary** about a teacher activity with an example of something a teacher has done in a lesson. These are designed to raise your awareness of what may be effective or less effective for embedding English. You are asked to reflect on the example and a commentary is provided at the end of the chapter.

Answers to quiz about English

1. How many people speak English in the world?
Estimates range from one in four to one in seven of the world's population speak English to some level. This includes those for whom English is a first language as well as those who speak English as a second or additional language.

2. Which of the following languages have contributed words to English: French, Norse, German, Czech, Gaelic?
The answer is, all of them. English is a notorious borrower from other languages and much of English draws on other languages.

3. How many different sounds are there in English?
There are 44 distinct sounds in English as opposed to 26 letters. The lack of one-to-one correspondence between sounds and letters provides many challenges to spelling and reading.

4. What percentage of the world's electronic information is stored in English?
It is estimated that about 80% of electronic information is stored in English. This suggests that the use of English for online purposes is an important area to address with learners.

3 Reading and listening – receptive skills

Reflective task

Think of three things that you have read or listened to in the last 24 hours – for example, a TV programme, a magazine article, a book, the back of a cereal packet. Think of each of them as a *text* (a piece of spoken or written language).

Now answer the following questions in relation to the three texts you have chosen. The questions will be addressed in some of the discussion that follows in this chapter.

1.   Did you have a reason for reading or listening?
2.   Did you take any information from the texts?
3.   Did you read or listen more than once?
4.   Did you understand every word that you heard or read?
5.   Did you read anything out loud?
6.   Did you do anything with the information you gained from the texts?

Introduction

Reading and listening are sometimes referred to as *receptive skills* because they involve processing text that we receive aurally, through hearing, or visually, through reading. It is useful to consider them together because many of the issues that arise for learners can be addressed this way. Your learners will need to be able to read and listen to texts you use in your subject lessons. However, there are some strategies you can use to develop their skills further so that they are more proficient readers and listeners and able to deal with more complex and longer texts.

You ought to be aware that there are different ways of reading and listening. None of these is more correct or more valuable; instead, it is important to determine which is appropriate to the texts you use in your subject area.

Reading/listening to get the 'gist' of it

This will be sufficient when your learners simply need to have an idea of an overarching issue. For example, they might read a number of evaluative texts or listen to someone evaluate a procedure in catering to get a view of whether something was generally positive or negative. The outcome would simply be a broad idea whether it was a good choice or not.

Reading/listening for general understanding

This is a little bit more intensive and requires the reader or listener to have an understanding of the main points. In classroom activities, is it tempting to have many activities which ask the learners for the 'main points', but it is worth considering whether the text needs to be processed in such detail.

Reading/listening for detailed understanding

Here the reader/listener is looking for a very specific thing or things. It may be looking at a set of instructions that have to be followed carefully. Or maybe they need to attend to particular details in a longer text.

Depending on the type of reading or listening required, learners will approach the text differently. For written texts, for example, learners can use headings and subheadings to find information without the need to read the whole text. This is a very effective reading strategy. However, learners may feel they have to read or listen *and* understand everything to undertake 'real' reading or listening. You can embed the development of English skills by showing them that there are different approaches and they should use whichever is appropriate to the context and task.

Types of text for the reflective task

In selecting your texts for the reflective task, you will have chosen them from a huge variety of available texts, both written and spoken, which we encounter in our everyday lives. Your selection will also have depended on where you made your choices. If you were at work, you no doubt would have had a different selection of texts to choose from than if you were at home, on holiday or elsewhere.

Your learners will also have experience of a range of texts, many of them familiar to you and many not so. Similarly, some of the texts you use in your subject classroom (readings, videos, etc.) may be familiar to your learners, but not all of them. Many of the texts you use will have specific subject language and are likely to be written in a less accessible way than the texts we typically read for pleasure. Your learners may not be familiar with the way such texts are organized or the best way to approach them to find the information they need. Bearing this in mind, it is a good idea to anticipate aspects of the text learners might have difficulty with. The example in Table 3.1 is of a classroom reading task. A teacher of business studies wants learners to read a job contract to prepare for a discussion on human resources practices. The difficulty with text type is highlighted, together with ideas for how you could support learners' reading.

Table 3.1

Possible difficulty	Solutions
Learners are unlikely to have read this type of text before.	**Before they read:** • Ask learners about reading other similar texts, e.g. phone contracts • Show contract headings (general duties, conditions of service) and discuss what might be in these sections and which sections are the important ones to read • Show examples of legalistic language they might encounter in the text

Purpose for reading or listening (Question 1 of the reflective task)

It is unusual to read or listen to something with no purpose in mind. There are exceptions of course: background music when you are cooking, reading ads in the station when you are waiting for the train. In general, we approach reading or listening to a text with a purpose; for example, to locate some specific information, to be entertained or to find instructions on how to do something. These purposes are our motivation for reading or listening.

The texts you use in your subject classroom do not have an intrinsic purpose for your learners. They may be aware that the information is useful for their subject, but without a clear purpose for reading or listening, these texts can become a classroom chore and reading or listening a burdensome activity potentially leading to disengagement.

The first solution to a potential lack of motivation is to contextualize the material and indicate its importance to learners. It is not really enough to simply say 'we're going to read ...' or 'we're going to listen to ...'. One way to engage learners with a text is to ask them to anticipate what might be in it based on their prior knowledge of the topic. This is also a good way to assess prior knowledge and to reactivate what learners already know. The example shown in Table 3.2 is of how a teacher might enhance the setting up of a listening activity.

Table 3.2

Activity	Suggested plan
Motor vehicle teacher says: 'We're going to watch a video about health and safety in the workshop' (then plays video)	• Teacher explains video is about health and safety in the workshop • Teacher asks learners to predict some topics they think might arise • Learners put forward ideas as to potential content of the video • Learners are asked to listen for topics they have missed that are important for health and safety

A second solution would be to have a *task* for learners to undertake *while* they are reading or listening. This strategy is considered in the next section.

Setting a task (Questions 2 and 3 of the reflective task)

As well as having a purpose for reading and listening, we usually draw some information from our text. This may be simply *what happens next* in our favourite TV programme, or it may be complex information that we need for a particular activity, such as a set of instructions for building something.

Our intended purpose will impact on the way we read or listen. In some instances, we may simply wish to have a general idea of the main content of a text; in others, we may need to read or listen more intensively, focusing on the detail. One of the skills we possess as proficient readers is the ability to make a decision on *how* we read or listen and adapt our approach accordingly.

In the classroom, learners may approach the text in different ways from one another. Learners may also adopt one of two default approaches, often as a result of the perceived difficulty of the text, particularly if it is long and complex. One reaction is to switch off because of the effort involved in trying to comprehend the text. The other default position is to try to understand everything about a text, but failing to do so because one cannot sustain the intensity of the reading or listening required.

One solution therefore is to set a task that reflects the nature of the approach learners should use with the text you are introducing. By doing this you are developing good habits by showing learners that there are different ways to read and that they should make their choice based on the purpose of their reading. Having a task also reflects the way we all read and listen naturally, in that we approach a text to get something out of it. Normally, we set our own task: 'what do I want to know?' When you introduce material to read or listen to, learners do not have in-built questions or things they want to take from the text, so you can help develop their reading and listening skills by giving them something to focus on.

This focusing task should be introduced *before* the learners read or listen, so that they adopt an approach that is appropriate to the text. It is essential that they know the task before they get the text or before the video is played. Asking them to simply read or listen and then posing them questions afterwards does not reinforce good reading or listening skills. Also, their first reading or hearing of the text could potentially be a waste of time, since they won't have known what they were reading or listening *for*. Types of tasks and the types of reading or listening they encourage are shown in Table 3.3.

Table 3.3

Type of task	Reading or listening approach it encourages
Comprehension questions	Detailed reading or listening
Summary/summary questions	General understanding of text
Yes/no or true/false	Looking for specific pieces of relevant information

In your subject classroom, it is tempting to stick to one type of task, for example: 'read this and summarize the main points'. But not every text will lend itself to this type of task. The other practice that is easy to slip into is simply asking the learners to read and listen and promising them some questions afterwards. This is not a good idea because it leaves the learners in a state of not knowing how they should read and listen, and they will likely revert to one of the default approaches of switching off or trying to understand everything.

A task will always be clearer if it is presented in written format and reinforced verbally. A good task will be clear and unambiguous. Learners should have access to the task before and during the reading or listening – it is too late to present the task after they have processed the text. This point is also relevant for note-taking when you are delivering a lecture or demonstration as part of your teaching. Lectures and demonstrations are just as much listening tasks. Learners should have a clear idea of how they should listen and what points they should focus on. For some learners, having a list of bullet points that are to be covered encourages effective listening and makes it more likely that they will learn from the activity.

When listening to an audio or video presentation, there are fewer opportunities to review or repeat it. Unlike a written text, learners usually only get one go. And although a recorded text could be repeated, you are unlikely to repeat a lecture or demonstration you have given! The ephemeral nature of spoken text means that it is even more important to have a clear task when listening than when reading. When you have sourced an interesting video related to your lesson topic, it is tempting to simply show it as a stimulus to motivate learners. However, it is still important to set some kind of task.

Embedding reminder

✔ Ensure any text is contextualized.
✔ Give the learners a purpose for reading/listening.
✔ Give them a task **before** they read or listen.
✔ Listening is more challenging, so a task is even more important.
✔ Vary the task – not always a summary or comprehension questions.
✔ Plan the task so that it is clear and unambiguous and reflects the type of reading or listening you want the learners to undertake.

Avoid

✗ 'Just read/listen to this and I'll ask you some questions afterwards.'

Unknown words (Question 4 of the reflective task)

It is highly likely that the texts you read contain some words that you do not completely understand. These might be highly technical words that are unfamiliar to you or words that do not form part of your everyday vocabulary. However, not being familiar with these words is unlikely to impact your comprehension of a text. You are unlikely to look such words up in a dictionary; instead, you will use your understanding of the rest of the text to make an educated guess as to the meaning of the unfamiliar words. This is a strategy used by proficient readers. It works if you have enough of a general understanding to make such an educated guess. However, if many of the words used are unfamiliar to you, you might struggle to work out the meaning of all of them.

Dealing with difficult words in the classroom can be done in different ways. One way is to encourage learners to ignore such words and try to gain a general understanding of the text. This is best achieved if the learners have a task that encourages them to read or listen for general understanding.

Another strategy is to highlight difficult key words before they read/listen. This can be done using vocabulary activities (Chapter 5) or simply by providing them with a glossary of words and definitions. The key is to choose those words that are likely to prevent learners from understanding the text if they do not know what they mean, rather than highlighting every possible challenging word.

Embedding reminder

✔ A key reading/listening strategy is being able to determine the meaning of words from the context in which they appear. Therefore, when learners encounter the reading or listening text for the first time:

Avoid

✗ 'I want you to read/listen to this and underline/note down all the words you don't understand.'

Reading aloud (Question 5 of the reflective task)

Unless you were thinking of a very specific context, such as reading a story to a child, you probably answered 'no' to Question 5. Reading aloud is not something we do often in our daily lives. However, the practice of reading texts aloud in class is quite common, but not always beneficial for the development of reading skills. When learners read aloud, they are often focused on individual words and how to say them. They are less likely to be focused on understanding the text, which is, after all, the purpose of reading.

There are other reasons you might ask learners to read aloud. For example, it can be a settling activity if the class has been quite active. It may also provide some support for the other students who are listening, as it can help them with their own ability to work out the individual words. For learners who are not confident readers, reading aloud can be difficult and potentially humiliating, and it won't contribute to the development of their reading skills. Use sparingly and think before doing it.

Embedding reminder

✔ Reading aloud does not generally help learners to read. It can also be very challenging and upsetting for some learners.

Avoid

✗ Asking learners to read texts aloud. Instead, set a task and ask them to read silently.

Using the information (Question 6 of the reflective task)

After accessing a text, we normally use the information we have acquired for some purpose. We may simply reflect on what we have read. We may use information to do something, such as accessing a train timetable online to plan a journey or following a set of instructions for a computer application. In earlier sections, we highlighted the importance of *purpose* for reading and listening. You may wish to present this purpose in terms of what the learners will *do* with the information after they have read or listened to it. For example, they may need the information to engage in a classroom discussion or to complete a written task.

Specific issues for learners with English as a second or other language

All of the strategies discussed so far will benefit learners for whom English is not their first language. However, there are additional things to be aware of. Table 3.4 highlights some of those additional challenges and offers some suggestions.

Embedding example 1

Below is a text that was used by an IT teacher to stimulate a discussion about online security. It is followed by a brief description of a lesson. Using the information presented in this chapter, evaluate the effectiveness of the lesson for the embedding of English reading skills development.

Several tech firms are urging people to change all their passwords after the discovery of a major security flaw. One blogging platform has advised the public to change their passwords everywhere – especially when using some high-security services like email, file storage and banking. There have been similar warnings about the use of social media sites.

Table 3.4

Additional challenges	Suggestions
The **context** of the text may be cultural in nature. For example, a job contract may have clauses that relate only to UK employment law	Ask the learners to share their own context. Acknowledge that things may not be the same in every country
Unknown words – there may be many unknown words and even if learners can work out what the words are, they may not comprehend their meaning	Scrutinize the text for words that have difficult meanings. For example, the expression 'jot this down' might seem very simple, but its meaning is very complex Give learners more vocabulary to research before they read or listen
Reading aloud is even more challenging, as learners have to focus on pronunciation as well as reading the word	Avoid!

It follows news that a product used to safeguard data could be compromised to allow eavesdropping. One of the most popular cryptographic libraries that is used to digitally scramble sensitive data as it passes to and from computer servers so that only the service provider and the intended recipients can make sense of it has recently been breached. If an organization employs this library, users see a padlock icon in their web browser – although this can also be triggered by rival products.

Those affected include one country's tax-collecting agency, which halted online services to safeguard the integrity of the information they held. However, experts stress that they have no evidence of cybercriminals having harvested the passwords and that users should check which services have fixed the flaw before changing their login.

Lesson procedure

- In groups, learners discuss examples of breaches of online security they or acquaintances have experienced. The class compares examples.
- The teacher shows a picture of a padlock icon and asks learners what this means to them in connection with internet security.

- Next, the teacher explains that they are going to look at an online news story about online security and that they will use this as the basis for a discussion later.
- The teacher shows a list of words from the text and asks the learners to explain any differences in meaning when used in IT and when used generally.
  - List: *safeguard, compromise, eavesdrop, scramble, icon, browser, integrity, platform*.
- The teacher gives learners three questions to find the answer to in the text.
  - Questions: What problem has been identified? What advice has been given? Is the danger genuine?
- The learners read and make notes. They then compare their answers in pairs before checking as a whole class.
- The teacher then asks the groups to use the same questions for another online security problem to prepare a brief case study that they will share with the whole class.
- Each group presents their case study and invites comments for discussion.

Evaluation of embedding reading skills development

- The teacher provided a clear context for the text, linking it to learners' own experience. This helps provide intrinsic motivation for reading.
- The learners were encouraged to predict the content of the text and therefore would have had some ideas in mind when they approached the text. This helps learners process the text and not become discouraged by unknown words.
- The teacher dealt with some key vocabulary that might cause difficulties in understanding the text. In addition, work on different meanings of words helps to extend learners' vocabulary within and outside the vocational area.
- The teacher set a clear task focusing on the general understanding of the text. Learners were encouraged to read for meaning.
- A follow-up task allowed learners to use the information they gathered from the text for a clear purpose. This reinforces the value of reading for learners.

Embedding example 2

The transcript of a short video used by a plumbing teacher to introduce a lesson on radiator valves is shown below. Identify some activities the teacher could use in the lesson to embed the development of listening skills. There are some suggestions in the commentary that follows.

Today we're going to look at thermostatic radiator valves, otherwise known as TRVs. They individually control the temperature in the room to an individual radiator. We'll be looking at the way they work and how they are different from other valves.

So how does a TRV work and what's the difference between that and a normal radiator valve? First of all, a normal radiator valve is simply a valve that shuts off the flow of hot water from the boiler to the radiator (shows picture), just like the tap on a bath tap. The main difference with a thermostatic radiator valve is that it automatically controls the amount of water going into a radiator according to the current heat of the room where it is located.

There are two main types of thermostatic radiator valve. One uses a spring that expands and contracts and one uses a wax jacket that does exactly the same. In the spring type valves we have a metal spring that is very susceptible to the temperature around it. If the room is cold, the metal will contract because that's what metal does when it's cold. Therefore, the valve will be open and hot water will be allowed to flow into the radiator. If the room is warm, the metal will expand because it is warm and the spring will be pushed down and the flow of hot water to the radiator will be stopped.

Commentary

Possible contextualization/prediction activities – to establish the purpose and motivation for listening

- Learners describe valves they already know and are then told the video will be about one type.
- Learners suggest 'top tips' for saving energy in household heating and are told the video will relate to managing energy consumption in the home.
- Learners are shown pictures of different valves and are asked to match names to the pictures. Learners are told they will be able to check their answers when viewing the video.

Possible activities for addressing unfamiliar words – to ensure learners focus on the meaning of the whole text

- Learners are given a list of words: *valve, spring, flow, tap, jacket,* and are asked to explain the connection between the words in relation to radiators.
- Learners are asked to decide how the following words relate to temperature control in a house: *shuts off, automatically, susceptible, contract, expand, control.*
- Learners are asked to provide opposites for the following words: *shut off, automatically, contract, susceptible.*

Possible tasks for learners while they are listening

- True/false – so that learners do not have too much written language to focus on while listening.

  Example: A TRV responds to the temperature of the room

  True / False

- Matching picture and text – reduces the reading load while listening. Learners match pictures of the different valves and pictures of the 'contract/expand' position of the spring to their labels.
- Questions on the content: What are the differences between TRVs and other valves? What happens in a cold room? What happens in a warm room? (These questions provide a reading and writing load and may detract from the listening activity.)

Further reading

Harmer, J. (2007) *The Practice of English Language Teaching* (4th edn.). Harlow: Longman. Provides some good discussion of the different processes involved in reading and listening and ideas for ways in which reading and listening can be facilitated for learners who have English as a second language.

Hughes, N. and Schwab, I. (2010) *Teaching Adult Literacy* Maidenhead: Open University Press.

4 The productive skills – writing and speaking

Reflective Task 1

Below is an extract of spoken English. Someone is explaining to a friend how to dye their hair at home.

What we need to do is to make the bathroom ready. Sometimes you get dye on the wall or on the floor and our parents get really cross. So these clean towels need to be out, out of the room, it's pretty serious if they're not, you know. What you can do is put these bits here on the side and this will catch it. If there's drips, you can't have drips.

- What do you think this extract might look like if it were a written rather than a spoken explanation?
- What differences might there be between the spoken and written versions.

At the end of the chapter, you will find an example written text and a commentary on possible differences.

Reflective Task 2

You are asked to write or speak about one of the following:

A letter of complaint   **A presentation**   **A report in your subject area**

Would you know how to go about such a task? For example, layout, structure, language use, and so on?

Some suggested answers are provided at the end of the chapter.

Introduction

This chapter focuses on writing and speaking. These two skills are dealt with together because they both require learners to produce language, and this suggests that similar strategies for embedding might be used to develop learners' proficiency. Speaking skills also feature in Chapter 6, where there is a specific focus on the needs of learners who have English as a second language.

Differences between spoken and written English (Reflective task 1)

One area of difficulty for learners is illustrated by this reflective task. When asked to produce written work, learners often 'write as they speak' and the resulting piece will not have the expected features of a written text. This commonly results in writing that does not have the formality required, either in the way it is structured or the language that is used.

A good idea, therefore, is to work with learners on recognizing the differences between spoken and written English so that they can choose language appropriate to the task at hand. This can be easy to implement in the classroom, as learners are often prepared for what they need to write through discussion of a particular topic in class. In order to embed the development of writing skills, the teacher needs to make explicit what changes are expected when the learners transfer their ideas into the written word.

Embedding example: formal language

On an environmental science course, students have undertaken some research on an airline company that has tried to promote the use of more environmentally friendly fuels. Having reported back, extracts from the contributions of one group are given below. The teacher uses these to prepare the learners to write the formal report on their research.

> *So we've just had a look at how SantosAir had been trying to get everyone to agree to this carbon neutral policy and how they've pushed for getting these new planes that reduce carbon emissions to be developed.* (Student 1)

> *They didn't actually use these new fuels when they were a working company, but they wanted to use them but didn't manage to. But we think they gave the whole thing the push it needed.* (Student 2)

> *We also found out that these new fuels can be used just like that, they don't need to change the engine, so you can't argue that it costs more.* (Student 3)

Embedding ideas

✔ The teacher takes notes during the discussion and then asks the learners to come up with more formal (writing) words for selected expressions from the spoken exchange. Some possible areas of focus are shown in Table 4.1.

Table 4.1

Discussion	Writing
Research expressions: We've just had a look at ... We also found out that ...	We have engaged in research into ... We have researched ... Our findings suggest that ... An outcome from the research is ...
Process words: They've pushed for ... They gave the whole thing the push	Implemented, encouraged an ethos of, promoted the concept
Formal alternatives: Change the engine, it costs more, they didn't manage to ...	Modify the engine, it is more expensive, they did not succeed in ...
Formal structures: They didn't actually ... but they ... They don't need to change ...	Although they ... However, ... Modification is not necessary ...

✔ This activity could be extended by videoing the discussion and asking learners to identify some of the more informal language used that they will need to incorporate into their report.
✔ The teacher could also simply present some alternative words and phrases similar to the chart above and ask learners to match formal and informal expressions.

The 'rules' of text – written and spoken (genre) (Reflective task 2)

When thinking about reflective task 2, you no doubt came up with some similar and some different answers to the ones suggested at the end of the chapter. The key point is that you were aware of the expectations for writing and speaking in these formats. You have some internal *rules* that provide you with information about the conventions used in these types of text. We often refer to a written or spoken text type as a *genre*.

These rules operate to create the social expectations of what a text will be like. Such rules are often reinforced in the educational setting by the expectations of regulatory bodies for qualifications. Course work or exam answers are expected to be in a certain format and follow specific conventions. Learners do not always have a good understanding of these conventions and in an educational setting, many of the genres (e.g. essays and presentations) will be unfamiliar to them.

An important part of developing learners' writing and speaking skills is making these rules of the written and spoken genre explicit to learners by raising their awareness of general rules and also those related to the expectations for a course of study, usually laid down by an awarding body.

How to raise awareness of the *rules* of writing and speaking

Many of the strategies you could use can be categorized into those that focus on the *process* of writing or speaking and those that focus on the *product*. Process-focused strategies follow the student through the preparation and revision of their work, providing guidance through reference to explicit rules, such as a checklist. Product-focused strategies provide an example of the genre and encourage learners to work out the rules so that they can apply them to their own writing or speaking. There is no definitive view regarding which of these strategies is better, but it is clear that certain strategies are more useful in certain situations as discussed below.

Process strategies

Activities that focus on the process use previously defined rules of writing or speaking a text. The learners work with their ideas and through a process of revision and checking, refine their text so that it complies with the conventions.

Embedding example: process focus

On a travel and tourism programme, the learners undertake a field trip to investigate the potential impact of the proposal to build a casino in the nearby coastal resort of Sumton. They are required to write a report and take part in a group discussion as part of their assessment for the module. The teacher provides guidance in the form of a checklist to support the writing and speaking skills development of the learners based on process strategies, i.e. learners have guidance for each stage of the writing or speaking *process*.

Prior to the field trip, the teacher provides the following guidance.

The report

Your report will need to cover the following areas/issues:
- *The history of the development of Sumton, identifying any key historical developments within the travel and tourism industry that have affected it.*

- *The main economic, environmental and social impacts of the proposed casino developments.*
- *The role that local and national government can play through funding or other initiatives to support the development.*
- *The report must contain clear sections for each of these points. The section headings should identify the main point of each of the sections.*
- *There should be a clear introduction and conclusion summarizing your ideas.*
- *Bullet points can be used for key points, but the main report must be written in prose.*
- *You should write the report in formal English.*

The group discussion

- *You should come together and discuss your findings in groups.*
- *Each person should present his or her findings for a maximum of five minutes.*
- *The group should then analyse their findings and clarify the key positive and negative impacts of the new casino.*
- *Ask questions about any findings where you feel clarification is necessary.*
- *Use positive language. You may disagree with findings, but do this using evidence from your own research.*

Embedding reminder

✔ After the field trip when learners are writing their report, the teacher encourages them to use the guidance to check their writing. Learners are encouraged to use the checklist to peer assess their work.

✔ During the group discussion, the teacher ticks each point on the checklist as the group successfully completes each step. The teacher writes a question mark against any area that is underdeveloped and notes down examples of where this happened.

Such guidance on writing and speaking genres is often readily available as part of the materials for teaching specific qualifications. It is common to find that the assessment criteria are based on meeting the writing and speaking expectations. A process approach is therefore commonly used. As an English embedding strategy, the important thing is that the 'rules' of structure and expectations are made explicit to learners before and during the process of writing or speaking. They can then monitor what they are producing against these rules.

These strategies work well with learners who already have some idea of different spoken and written genres and for whom the guidance will be clear. For example, the guidance to 'write in formal language' or 'use positive language' is easy to follow if you know what they mean. The teacher can extend the guidance by providing some examples of that language. Another approach, however, is to provide the learners with a *model* of how this is done. Such an approach is a product-focused strategy.

Embedding example: product focus

In the same scenario as the one above, another teacher adopts a different approach. Guidance as to what areas will need to be covered is given prior to the field trip as in the approach above.

Before learners write their report, the teacher provides an extract from an example report and asks them questions to draw their attention to features of the genre.

> *Sumton has over the years felt the impact of development and change within the tourism industry, much of which has been of a negative nature. Lack of investment within the area has left Sumton looking very old and tired. Failure to respond to the changing needs of the tourist has seen a very prosperous coastal resort become a shadow of its former self. Efforts are now being made to rejuvenate this resort and to target specific tourist groups.*

XXXXX

> *Against this background the local council has submitted a proposal to build a new casino funded entirely from private sources. Is has already engaged a partner which has agreed to provide 50% of the funds and it is currently seeking another partner to make up the rest. In a recent announcement on its website, the council stated the following advantages of the new proposal:*

> * *Regeneration of a part of the town that has been derelict for some years.*
> * *Improved transport infrastructure.*
> * *An increase in the number of tourists and therefore increased spending in other resort areas.*

Questions

1. What is the purpose of the first paragraph?
2. Is the information in the first paragraph general or specific to what has been researched?

3. What heading should be used to replace **XXXXX** to make the following section clear?
4. Why are bullet points used?
5. Find formal equivalents for the following expressions in the text: *There's been no money put in. A lot has been bad. People are doing something now.*

An approach using a model has some advantages over a process approach. It can lead to more discovery learning, as the learners have to work out some of the features of the writing for themselves. This can increase the likelihood that they will remember the features. A model can also be reassuring for learners who are struggling with a particular genre, as it gives them something to imitate at the beginning. It can also be useful for learners who simply struggle with 'where to start'. A disadvantage is that it can close down the development of ideas if learners try to imitate a model too closely, limiting the potential for them to develop their own texts.

Another possibility is to use a negative model – a poorly executed model for learners to identify what went wrong. Using such a model helps learners to identify the key features of a successful text. In the example above, where learners have to engage in a group discussion, another approach would be to show a video of a group discussion that did not go well. Awareness-raising questions, like those for the written report, can be employed:

Embedding idea

✓ Learners watch a video of a group discussion that was unsuccessful and ended in a group argument. They make notes on the following:

Questions

1. Who spoke most in the group?
2. Why did some members speak more than others?
3. Can you identify examples of unclear points presented by the participants?
4. Are there examples of negative language use?
5. Who was the most effective in maintaining a positive discussion and what strategies did they use to do this?

Embedding example: writing frames

For learners who struggle with writing and the new genres they are required to tackle, a teacher can provide a model in the form of a writing frame that makes the structure and language very explicit. Some writing frames provide a diagrammatic flow chart of what the learner should write. An even more prescriptive frame, based on the model report above, might look something like the following:

> *Sumton has over the years _____, much of which has been of a negative nature. Lack of investment within the area has_____. Failure to respond to the changing needs of the tourist has seen a very prosperous coastal resort_____. Efforts are now being made to _____.*

Although this may seem as if you are writing the report for them, for learners who lack confidence in writing, such a writing frame may be a great help in getting them started and avoiding the anxiety related to the 'blank page' in front of them. You could, for example, adopt such a strategy at the very beginning of a programme of study or when introducing a new written genre.

Embedding reminder

✔ Remember that learners will not always know the conventions for writing or speaking the text you are asking them to complete.

✔ Some learners need a lot of support and may benefit from a very prescriptive frame at the start of their programme of study.

Texts that make sense: discourse

In the next chapter, we look at grammar and accuracy in writing. Here, we consider the way written and spoken texts 'hang together' so that they make sense. The two main features of texts that make sense are well-organized content (coherence) and the use of language that makes links between different parts of the text (cohesion), like a kind of language 'glue' that brings parts of the text together.

A key part of written text organization is the use of paragraphs or sections and, where appropriate, section headings. For many learners this can be a challenge, and an approach taken by some learners is simply to make a break when they have filled an arbitrary portion of the page. An important focus of the embedding of writing is highlighting the use of paragraphs and effective use of the topic sentence: the first sentence of the paragraph, which states what the content of the paragraph will be.

Below is a text produced by a learner on a catering course to describe an experiment they designed to test taste and flavour. The text does not hang together very well. Some areas of coherence and cohesion are identified in Table 4.2, which is followed by a suggested improved text.

Taste and flavour test

Prepare three sets of drinks using three different flavoured waters. Add red food colouring and put the drinks in identical containers. We would suggest using lemon and lime, peach and red grapefruit.

The food colouring will mean that all the drinks look alike.

Present the drinks in the identical containers and use non-sequential codes to label each container. We will ask everyone in the group to test the three different drinks and guess the flavour and then think about the effect of the appearance.

Table 4.2

Coherence (the content/text organisation)	Cohesion (the language 'glue')
Topic goes from flavours to food colouring, then back to flavours All food colouring content belongs in the same paragraph One-sentence paragraph does not belong on its own	Could do with more sequential signposting (e.g. 'First', 'after that') Repetition of 'food colouring' rather than using 'it', or 'container' instead of 'each one' Possible overuse of 'and' as a link between sentences. Lacks variety

Suggested alternative

Method

Prepare three sets of drinks using three different flavoured waters, for example, lemon and lime, peach and red grapefruit. Then add red food colouring so that all the samples look alike. Present the drinks in identical containers using non-sequential codes to label each one.

Each person will test the three different drinks and guess the flavour. Additionally, they will be asked to consider the effect of the appearance of the drink on their judgement.

The revised text is more coherent in that each paragraph has a distinct topic focus. The focus is explained in the first sentence in each paragraph – the *topic* sentence. Within the paragraphs, each topic is contained. Language is used to show sequence and repetition is avoided.

The writing and, to a certain extent, speaking skills needed to produce a text that is coherent and cohesive often need to be developed in lessons. Here are some ideas on how that can be done with your subject specialist teaching.

Embedding ideas

✓ **Idea 1 – paragraphs**
Present a list of bullet point ideas to learners and ask them to organize the ideas into paragraphs. Discuss different variations and explore why things could be organized in different ways.

✓ **Idea 2 – paragraphs**
Jumble a model text or cut up a text and ask learners to rearrange it so that it makes sense. For example, with the text used above, a jumbled version might look as follows:

Each person will test the three different drinks and guess the flavour. Prepare three sets of drinks using three different flavoured waters, for example, lemon and lime, peach and red grapefruit. Present the drinks in identical containers using non-sequential codes to label each one. Additionally, they will be asked to consider the effect of the appearance of the drink on their judgement. Then add red food colouring so that all the samples look alike.

✓ **Idea 3 – paragraphs and topic sentences**
Rewrite a text to remove the topic sentence from each paragraph. Give the learners a list of the topic sentences and ask them to match them to the paragraphs.

✓ **Idea 4 – learner work**
Ideas 1–3 can be done with learners' work in its draft stages. Learners can bring in their work and test out their paragraphing by asking their peers to reassemble the texts. Any difficulty encountered will suggest a lack of coherence.

✓ **Idea 5 – cohesion**
Provide the learners with some simple sentences on a topic they will need to write about. Task them with combining the sentences into as few sentences as possible so that they use cohesive devices to link sentences together. (This activity is explored further in the next chapter on sentences and words.)

✓ **Idea 6 – coherence in speaking**
Similar ideas as above can be used with recordings of spoken texts (presentations, discussions, etc.).

✓ **Idea 7 – coherence and cohesion in speaking**
Work with learners on a scripting approach to a spoken text. For example, to prepare learners for a group discussion on safety in the workplace, one teacher helped a learner complete the prompt sheet in Table 4.3.

Table 4.3

Content (coherence)	How I say it (cohesion)
Need to mention:	Introduce points:
Physical environment – falling objects, trailing wires, on-site building work	The first/second point I'd like to make is ...
	In my opinion/From my perspective...
Food hygiene – food preparation areas, toilets and hand washing facilities, pest control	Another/further point is ...
	Agree/disagree:
	I don't quite agree/I'm not in favour of/I totally agree
Equipment – safety testing, installation, replacement policy	Conclusion:
	To sum up/Taking all the points into consideration ...

Working with writing and speaking for learners who have English as a second language

For the most part, the issues and strategies discussed so far will be applicable to learners who do not have English as a first language. There may be additional challenges to consider. For example, when dealing with written and spoken genres, learners might be very familiar with conventions used in their own language and so they may need to relearn new conventions for writing and speaking in English. It is good to engage them in a discussion of the comparative conventions to raise not just their awareness but your own too.

As a general strategy, it is worth remembering that for the productive skills of writing and speaking, ESOL learners will often require more time because they need to prepare both ideas and language. This is the case in particular for speaking activities. It is important to allow sufficient preparation time and not assume that learners will be able to immediately participate effectively in a group discussion, as they may need more time for language processing in addition to ideas processing.

Some of the difficulties that ESOL learners may experience include sentence level grammar in writing and pronunciation in speaking. Specific ideas to support grammar development are discussed in the next chapter and speaking and pronunciation are discussed in Chapter 6.

Correcting written work

The strategies considered up to now in this chapter have been mainly focused on embedding the development of writing and speaking in lessons. However, there is also an opportunity for embedding the development of writing in the way you approach the correction of learners' written work.

Depending on the requirements of your course programme, you may be asked to correct the language quality in the writing of your learners, but it is also possible you will not. Some qualifications require assessors to focus entirely on the content and as long as the necessary points are included, the quality of writing is immaterial. However, not making any comment on the writing is a missed opportunity for developing your learners' English writing skills.

Teaching decisions about correction

Regardless of the requirements of your programme of study, you will need to make decisions about what and when to correct the language in your learners' work. Many teachers adopt the default approaches of either correcting nothing or focusing heavily on spelling, punctuation and grammar (SPaG). Both of these approaches may be appropriate, but it is good if they are adopted in a principled manner with thought for the development of the individual learner.

It is also important to remember that you are now at the end of a chapter focusing on writing, where little has been said about spelling, grammar or punctuation. This should indicate that there are other aspects of writing that are important to comment on, such as text organization and use of language that links the text together, as well as working within the conventions of the genre. The next chapter has a specific focus on spelling, grammar and punctuation, and consideration is given to correction decisions in these areas. Here, we look at some general ideas for effective correction of written English.

Embedding ideas: correcting written work

✓ Alternate comments on spelling, punctuation and grammar with comments on text features (paragraphing, topic sentences, etc.). This will help both you and the learners to appreciate the value of different aspects of writing.

✓ Focus on repeated errors in a piece of work if there are a lot of errors. Learners can then focus on important areas that are hindering effective writing and will not be overwhelmed by having to work on too many aspects. This will require an acceptance on the part of the teacher that it isn't always a good idea to correct errors!

✓ Use highlighter pen to indicate errors. This avoids additional writing on the page that can be overwhelming and difficult to discriminate for some learners.

✓ Use a simple code for identifying error (PR = paragraph, SP = spelling, etc.) and encourage learners to use the code to self-correct. This can be most effective if used on draft work or where learners have an opportunity to resubmit work and there is an incentive to work with the code.

✓ Conduct an error quiz by collecting examples of anonymized errors from the class. Learners then compete to make as many corrections as possible.

✓ For ESOL learners, some errors in written work may be due to a poor understanding of English language structure. Beware of simply correcting the error without knowing why it was made (see Chapter 5).

Embedding example: correction of written work

A learner on a science programme is researching a new energy source. The extract below is from their written work. The teacher has underlined some errors and written a comment. Evaluate the correction strategy in the light of your reading in this chapter.

Methane hydrate is like ice crystals with natural methane gas locked inside. They are formed through a combinnation of cold and high pressure. They are found mainly on the edge of continental shelves. This is where the seabed drops sharply away into the ocean floor and where it is deep. Also the deposites of these compounds are enormous.

Estimates suggests that there is about the same ammount of carbon in methane hydrates as there is in all other organic carbon store on the planet so there is more energy in methane hydrates than in all the world's oil, coal and gas together.

Teacher comment

You need to use your spelling checker for your writing. There are a lot of spelling mistakes in this essay. Your writing doesn't flow very well.

Evaluation of teacher's approach

- There are some spelling errors in the text. However, two of them (*suggests* and *store*) are actually grammatical errors and could indicate that the learner has some difficulties with verb forms rather than spelling.
- The idea of 'flow' is not helpful. The learner probably does not know how to make the writing flow better. This is a vague term and could mean a number of things.
- The issue of paragraphing is not addressed. The final sentence in the first paragraph would be a good topic sentence in the second paragraph.
- The use of 'they' and 'this' in the first paragraph does not help the text hang together. It is unclear whether the learner is talking about ice crystals or gas. The confusion with singular and plural in 'estimates suggests' indicates that the learner is not really sure either.
- In some ways, the spelling errors impact *less* on the effectiveness of the writing than some of the text organization issues. However, the learner is given the message that the main area to work on is their spelling.

Embedding reminder: correction of written work

✓ You do not always have to correct every error in a learner's work; you should decide what is appropriate.
✓ Avoid being drawn into the 'easy' errors to spot – mainly spelling, punctuation and grammar. Some text organization difficulties are more important to work on.
✓ Encourage self and peer correction of all aspects of writing.

Embedding task

Table 4.4 shows an extract from a teacher's lesson plan on a hair and beauty programme of study. The class has considered the advantages and disadvantages of different tanning products. The extract relates to the final lesson activity.

Table 4.4

Content and teacher activity	Learner activity	Resources	Embedding English
Producing a leaflet to summarize points on tanning products. Teacher asks learners in groups to produce a leaflet	Learners work in groups of four and produce a leaflet	Paper/pens	Learners work on producing a leaflet that can be completed at home

As it is currently planned, this part of the lesson provides an opportunity for embedding of English writing skills, but the teacher has not embedded English. What would the teacher need to do to ensure that the development of writing skills was embedded in the lesson?

Check the commentary at the end of the chapter.

Reflective task 1: spoken and written English – example written text

Table 4.5

Spoken text	Possible written text
What we need to do is to make the bathroom ready. Sometimes you get dye on the wall or on the floor and our parents get really cross. So these clean towels need to be out, out of the room, it's pretty serious if they're not, you know. What you can do is put these bits here on the side and this will catch it. If there's drips, you can't have drips.	Prepare the bathroom first to avoid any spills that will annoy your parents. For example, any clean linen needs to be taken out of the bathroom, because otherwise this could result in difficulties. Place something on the side so that any drips are caught. You should not have any drips of dye.

Differences between spoken and written text

1. Spoken language is usually less formal. This has an impact on sentence structure and words used (*make ready/prepare*; *it's pretty serious if they're not/this could result in*). The level of formality is often called the *register*.
2. Written language is well formed with no need for repair or correction. Spoken language allows for reformulation and repetition (*need to be out/ out of the room*; *If there's drips/you can't have drips*).
3. Spoken language may be more vague or less specific because it can usually be accompanied by a visual demonstration of what is meant (*What you can do is put these bits here on the side*).
4. There is more tolerance of grammatical inaccuracies in spoken English (*If there's drips*).
5. Spoken language can contain fillers: words or phrases that have no real meaning but 'fill' the conversation (*you know*).

Reflective task 2: text type (genre) – suggested features

Table 4.6

A letter of complaint	A presentation	A report in your subject area
Opening and closing conventions (Dear Mr/Ms X, yours faithfully. etc.)	Use visuals with key points to accompany what is said. Introduction sets out main points	This may vary according to subject area, but likely to include:
First paragraph introduces problem; final paragraph proposes solution	Conclusion summarizes what is said	An introduction that sets out topic. Developing paragraphs and conclusion that summarizes findings
Use of descriptive language for feelings (annoyed, distressed, etc.)	Possible use of question and answer throughout	Possible use of figures and data
Conditional structures (If you are unable to resolve ... I will/I would be grateful if you could ...)	Language that points forwards and backwards (As I mentioned previously, I'd now like to consider ...)	Section headings
		Passive structures (X was found to be the best ...)

Commentary on lesson

- The teacher would need to highlight the key features of the genre 'leaflet'.
- A process-focused approach would simply be to list the key features of a leaflet.
- A product-focused approach would be to use other leaflets and ask the learners to identify key features.
- The teacher should include a focus on the language of leaflets. This often involves the use of simple sentences with imperative forms: *do this, take this*, etc.
- Some attention should be paid to how to make the text coherent. For a leaflet, the use of headings and subheadings is very important. This could be highlighted by looking at other examples.

5 Sentences and words

Reflective task

There is one error in each of the following sentences. Can you find them?

1. Could you confirm who you had arranged to meet today?
2. The bad weather meant that there were less people than expected at the event.
3. We missed you at the party, where was you?
4. The economic downturn continues to effect purchasing power.
5. Several student's handed in their work late.
6. He fractured a cup.

You can check your answers at the end of the chapter

Introduction: interesting things about sentences and words

This chapter looks at different ways of focusing on learners' use of words and sentences in both their written and spoken English. Noticing and correcting errors like the ones in the reflective task above is one way of encouraging your learners to be more *accurate* in their use of language. However important this may be, it is unlikely learners will be enthused or motivated if this is the only focus you have.

Thus the chapter is designed to show you some of the potentially more interesting aspects of words and sentences so that these can be the basis of the strategies you use in the classroom. Information is provided about English spelling, grammar and punctuation, as well as some further reading for those of you interested in reading more widely. There are a number of suggestions for classroom activities to help engage learners and make them more language aware and language curious, something that is likely to foster a more long-term improvement of their English skills.

The role of SPaG (spelling, punctuation and grammar)

In order to complete the above reflective task, you will have used your knowledge of certain language 'rules'. The errors you noticed break these rules and that is why they are labelled mistakes. Language is bound by rules and we cannot simply string random words together and create sentences that have meaning. Some of the rules you used to identify the errors are rules about spelling, punctuation and grammar, sometimes shortened to SPaG.

When completing the task, you may have felt that some of the rules seemed more 'important' than others. Or it could be that the rules that applied are more important in written language, which has a formal purpose, such as a job application or a letter of complaint. In the sentences in the reflective task, the errors in 1, 2 and even 3 are part of many people's everyday language use. These so-called 'errors' have become common usage in the way we speak and even write English. There have been suggestions, for example, that the word 'whom' might be disappearing from English, although in sentence 1 it is the grammatically correct form to use.

There is much debate about whether we should simply accept these changes in language use and embrace new ways of using language, which many people view as incorrect English. However much we may discuss the merits of change, there are many contexts where accuracy is important and you need to prepare your learners for those contexts: the workplace, formal study and formal roles in society. Value is placed on accuracy, particularly in writing, which means the more accurate the English is, the more seriously the piece of writing will be viewed and the more successful the writer considered to be. In formal situations, accuracy in spoken language is also important and an error like the one in sentence 3 might disadvantage the speaker because it would impact on the evaluation the listener makes both of what is said and of the person who says it.

On the other hand, in our classroom practice it is important to consider the temptation to use a focus on SPaG as a punitive tool where the teacher works carefully through every error a learner has made in written work and corrects it. This approach can be extremely demotivating and may simply be a continuation of the learner's prior experience of being labelled a failure at English. It is possibly easier for the teacher to notice and correct SPaG errors because, for the most part, the rules are unambiguous and easy to apply. In Chapter 4 on writing, we looked at some of the principles of deciding what to correct and the importance of looking at work with paragraphs and texts. The overarching idea is that some judgement must to be made on the part of the teacher as to how much emphasis should be placed on accuracy at any particular time.

It is also empowering for learners to discuss this issue, as it raises awareness that a focus on accurate language will benefit them. Below are some classroom activities you could employ to do this.

Embedding ideas

✓ Use an activity like the reflective task above. Ask learners to correct obvious and less obvious errors and then rank them in importance.

✓ Show examples of a task completed with various levels of accuracy (e.g. a job application), and ask them to rate the candidates for interview.

✓ Show an example of a text from your vocational context with some errors in it. Discuss the impact of the errors – some may be irrelevant.

✓ Work across formal and informal language. Ask learners to transform a verbal report, a written report, dialogue reported in a letter, etc.

✓ Make use of language in a text to highlight the boundaries of inaccurate language use and how much can/cannot be understood with little SPaG.

Interesting things about grammar

It is easy to think that you know very little about grammar because you are not always able to explain grammar rules or use terminology to describe language. For example, you may not have been completely familiar with the terms used in the answers to the reflective task. In fact, you likely have a very good knowledge of the grammar of English, but you know it *tacitly*, using it to produce language that communicates meaning. In order to support your learners, it is necessary to have some *explicit* knowledge of grammar, which will help you to recognize why learners are having the difficulties they are and suggest ways they could improve. It is not necessary to be a grammar expert, but it helps to look at an accessible grammar book (see suggestions in *Further reading*), discuss areas with specialist colleagues or simply reflect on your own language use and try to work out language patterns. Below we address three areas that cause learners problems and provide some ideas for addressing them in your classroom.

Word order

English has quite a fixed word order for sentences compared with other languages. The basic word order is:

Subject (does something) + **Verb** (the doing word) + **Object** (has something done to it)

Example:

The dog bit the man.

Changing the word order in English has a dramatic impact, which is not the case in other languages:

> *The man bit the dog* – different meaning
> *Bit man dog the the* – no meaning

Simple sentences use this basic word order consistently and most learners are proficient users of this pattern of sentence construction. This proficiency encourages them to stay in the comfort zone of simplicity, which is often a problem when their programme of study requires more complex written work.

When learners wish simply to vary the way they write sentences, they may not have control of what it is they would like to write or say. For example, if they want to talk about processes, the usual way to do this is to make what is called a *passive* structure:

Examples:

> *Wine is produced in Chile.*
> *Forty cars can be transported at one time.*

In these sentences, there is no subject and the object is at the beginning of the sentence.

To create effect or impact, we sometimes move things around:

Examples:

> *However much you pay …*
> *Never has the exchange rate been so volatile.*

A reluctance to use alternative structures and errors in learners' use may simply be due to the desire to stay within the comfort zone of simple sentences.

The verb and its tenses

The verb or doing word in sentences is a word that changes according to its use. Nouns change too – if they are made plural an 's' is usually added – but these changes are limited and fairly regular. Verbs change according to the person of the subject, this is why *was you* is an error. When the person is 'you', the verb should be 'were'.

Verbs also change significantly when they refer to different times. We call the different verb forms for different times *tenses*. Look at the sentences below and think about the time they might refer to:

1. I <u>am buying</u> a red bag.
2. I <u>bought</u> a red bag.
3. I <u>will buy</u> a red bag.

Generally speaking, 1 refers to the present time, 2 to the past and 3 to the future. The difference in the way the verb is spelled and whether it is formed of one or two words is challenging for all learners. There are fairly standard rules for spelling the different parts of the verb, including adding '-ing' and '-ed' to form present and past. These rules prove useful to learners.

For learners who have English as a second language, there are significant challenges in the way English uses verbs to relate to different times. Consider the sentences below and the time(s) they refer to:

1. I <u>buy</u> a red bag.
2. I <u>was buying</u> a red bag.
3. I <u>have bought</u> a red bag.
4. I <u>am buying</u> a red bag.

This time sentence 1 could indeed refer to the present, but it could equally refer to a habit, something I do once a week and therefore refer to past, present and future. Sentence 2 could refer to an intention in the past that was unfulfilled, or an action that was interrupted by 'when I noticed I'd forgotten my purse'. Sentence 3 could be a past action but also a reference to the present, saying 'I now have a red bag'. Sentence 4, which we identified earlier as present, could well be a future intention – I'm going to buy one.

Confused? The complexities of the English tense system are also a challenge because learners often contrast English with the tense system in their first language. Grammar books for ESOL learners provide good clarification of the different tenses. It is important for the teacher to realize that an error that may appear as a spelling issue might actually indicate a lack of understanding of the meaning or formation of the specific tense. Some examples of errors from ESOL learners include:

> *The process is been developed for a long time.*
> *The examples have change in the last batch.*
> *Does the outcome matches the predicted result?*

In the examples above, simply correcting the verb as a spelling mistake is not the most helpful thing to do. Learners should be advised to check the way the verb in that specific tense is formed. It is also helpful if learners are aware of the name of the tenses. Most grammar books (see list at the end of this chapter) can easily be self-accessed by learners.

Complexity in sentences

Where many learners struggle in their writing, and to a certain extent in their speaking, is in their ability to construct more complex sentences and move away from a reliance on the simple sentence of subject + verb + object. Consider the extract of writing below from a student on a hospitality course. It is perfectly correct, but lacks complexity.

> *Customer service is important. You must treat the customer in a welcoming manner. You need to be polite all the time. They will come into your business. You have to greet them in a friendly way. You should introduce yourself and you should ask them how they are. They might be comparing your business to another one. You must make a good impression. They could leave and choose another business.*

The issue with the text above is not SPaG, but a reluctance or inability to produce more complex sentences. Complex sentences have two or more parts (or clauses) linked in a more complex way than simply using 'and' or 'but'. Examples are given below using some of the sentences from the learner's work above.

> *They might be comparing your business to another one, therefore you must make a good impression.*

> *You must make a good impression because they might be comparing your business to another one.*

> *Introducing yourself and asking how they are means you make a good impression.*

> *In order to greet them in a friendly way you should introduce yourself and ask them how they are.*

Complexity in the examples above is achieved through the use of *linking* constructions (*therefore, because, in order to*) and by using some different sentence constructions: *By doing x …*

Embedding example

There are ways to encourage learners to write more complex sentences. Some examples are given below using this text from the nutrition module of a Catering course.

> *In food, carbohydrates, fats, vitamins and minerals are the main nutrients. Each nutrient has a different purpose.*

Proteins

You need proteins for your growth and the repair of cells in the body. Animal products such as meat, fish, cheese, milk and eggs are all good sources of protein. However, you can also get protein from vegetable sources such as soya-bean products, pulses and nuts.

Carbohydrates

You need to consume carbohydrates to give your body energy. There are two types of carbohydrates: starch and sugar. Starch is mainly found in cereals such as potatoes, pasta and flour, whereas sugar is found in fruit, vegetable, honey, milk and malt products.

Fats

You need fats to provide more concentrated sources of energy and to help insulate the body in cold temperatures. There are two main types of fat: saturated fats and polyunsaturated fats. The former comes from animal sources such as butter and lard, while the latter comes from vegetable sources, such as sunflower oil.

Embedding ideas

✓ **Idea 1**

Once learners have read the text and understand the content, the teacher asks the learners to underline the words that are used to connect/glue/link the different part of the sentences together (*such as, however, whereas, former/latter, : (colon)*).

Alternatively, the teacher highlights these words and asks the learners to identify their purpose. This can result in more discussion of the meaning of the linking devices. For example, 'however' suggests a contrast or contradiction; 'such as' introduces an example. The learners can then be tasked with using the same linking devices in a piece of writing on vitamins and minerals.

✓ **Idea 2**

The teacher gives the learners simple sentences that could be made into a more complex text. For example:

Carbohydrates provide energy.
There are two types of carbohydrates.
Starch is a type of carbohydrate.
Sugar is also a type of carbohydrate.

> The learners then have to construct a more complex text. An element of competition can be added by seeing which student can combine the most elements into the smallest number of sentences.
>
> ✓ **Idea 3**
>
> Idea 2 could also be used as follow-up feedback on initial learner statements about a particular topic. Learners may 'shout out' ideas or write down a 'shopping list' of ideas that will typically take the form of a list of simple sentences. By challenging them to compress this into a small number of more complex sentences, it will stretch their grammatical competence and benefit both their writing and speaking.

Interesting things about punctuation – it's more than just the apostrophe!

Punctuation is another area where over-correction by teachers can have a negative effect on learner confidence and engagement with the development of their language skills. Punctuation can impact significantly on meaning and therefore accuracy is often important. Consider the examples below, one with commas and the other with apostrophes.

Woman without her man is helpless. (Woman is helpless)
Woman, without her, man is helpless. (Man is helpless)

Place the metal sheet's sharper edge against the marker. (Use one sheet)
Place the metal sheets' sharper edge against the marker. (Use more than one sheet)
Place the metal sheets sharper edge against the marker. (Inaccurate, not clear how many sheets)

However, such ambiguity in sentences and potential for confusion seems rare compared with the strength of focus that is sometimes placed on the use of commas, apostrophes and other punctuation devices, particularly in the correction of written work. Perhaps consideration should be given to the frequency of such errors and the impact of the inaccurate use of punctuation on the effectiveness of the piece of writing. On occasion, we may wish to leave a stray apostrophe uncorrected! If this is something that fills you with horror, then by all means continue to correct any inaccurate use. But try to balance this with a focus on some other aspects of writing.

Embedding example

A potentially more interesting way to focus on punctuation is through discussion of its use within a text rather than a review of the 'rules', which many learners will have revisited many times before without having had much impact on their writing.

Table 5.1 shows an extract from a learner text from a course on international marketing. You could also use a published text. The learner is discussing a report they have read on brand colour. The text on the left is with punctuation and that on the right is without (apart from full stops and capital letters) as rewritten by the teacher.

Table 5.1

In a recent study, participants from two	1	In a recent study participants from two
groups made up of two different	2	groups made up of two different
nationalities were asked to discuss	3	nationalities were asked to discuss
their perceptions of Carrera's	4	their perceptions of Carreras
chocolate and the colour of its	5	chocolate and the colour of its
packaging: Blue – a colour that	6	packaging. Blue a colour that
Carrera's was intending to register as a	7	Carreras was intending to register as a
trademark. Asked about blue, the first	8	trademark. Asked about blue the first
group made associations with style,	9	group made associations with style
sophistication, youth and femininity.	10	sophistication youth and femininity.
The second group, on the other hand,	11	The second group on the other hand
talked of a warm, old, quiet colour,	12	talked of a warm old quiet colour
serious, a little sad, but dignified.	13	serious a little sad but dignified.
These perceptions of the packaging	14	These perceptions of the packaging
colour affected perceptions of the	15	colour affected perceptions of the
product: In one country Carrera's was	16	product In one country Carreras was
seen to be luxurious, stylish, expensive	17	seen to be luxurious stylish expensive
and classy, whilst in the other the	18	and classy whilst in the other the
brand was perceived as warm, friendly,	19	brand was perceived as warm friendly
but essentially poor and low in quality.	20	but essentially poor and low in quality.

Embedding ideas

✔ Learners are given the text on the left and asked to highlight punctuation marks and discuss their purpose. This works best if some learners in the group are confident about using punctuation in their writing.

✔ Learners are given the text on the left and asked to write two 'rules' for the use of commas (lists – lines 9 and 10; contrasting linking words – lines 11 and 18), one 'rule' for using apostrophe (brand names) and one for use of colons (introduces an example of something that has been explained – lines 6 and 16).

✓ Learners are given the text on the right and asked to add appropriate punctuation. They self-correct using the example on the left and then discuss similarities and differences. It is important that they see there is often some discrepancy in the way punctuation, particularly commas, is used while maintaining accuracy.

✓ As above, learners correct the punctuation in the text on the right and are then asked to rank the different punctuation in terms of its importance in the text. The learners may conclude that the use of commas with 'whilst' and 'on the other hand' is not as important, as the words themselves tdo the job of indicating the contrast. The commas in the listing are quite important.

Interesting things about words

The final part of our SPaG acronym is 'spelling', a feature that is associated with individual words. Although a focus on accurate spelling is important, there are many more interesting things about words than how they are spelled. So let us look at these first. There are some ideas for spelling focus at the end of this section.

Meaning is interesting

Words and phrases (groups of words) have meaning, which is why we can construct language by putting them together in a particular order (grammar). Having a specific focus on words is usually called focusing on *vocabulary* and there is likely to be a range of words that are very specific to your subject area which learners need to learn on your programme of study. Learners are more likely to be engaged, motivated and able to learn if you focus on what is interesting – i.e. meaning – rather than what is mundane – i.e. spelling.

Core meaning and additional meaning

All words will have a general meaning that most of us understand and other, more subjective meanings, which are individual to us or to a group of people. Let us look at the word used for a common piece of classroom equipment: 'desk'.

The core meaning of this word would be a structure at which someone can sit and use in some way for writing/doing their work in class. However, for each individual there will be multiple additional meanings – made of wood, metal, other material, for one or more people, like a table or a hand rest attached to a chair, etc.

The word 'desk' is a relatively straightforward word to describe an object and yet it can have many different meanings or *connotations*. Many words have even more potential for multiple meanings. If we take the word 'warm' to describe the weather, each individual will have different thresholds for when they consider the weather to be warm.

The multiplicity of meaning adds to the richness of language and is a very satisfying area to explore with learners. Some suggestions on how to do this within your subject specialism can be found in the *Embedding ideas* box below.

Relationships between words are interesting

Another area of great interest is the way words from the same field relate to one another. Look at the groups of words in Table 5.2 and try to describe their relationship.

Table 5.2

Group 1	*inform, information, informative*
Group 2	*chilly, cold, freezing*
Group 3	*vehicle, car, tractor, van*
Group 4	*wacky, strange*

The most obvious relationship might relate to the words in group 1 because there is a similar visual pattern and a clear derivation of words from the verb (inform) to the noun (information) to the adjective (informative). This is a relationship of structure and is probably less interesting to learners than some of the other groups.

The group 2 words have a relationship of *degree*. Each word represents a value of coldness on a scale, which might be subjective. There is potential for discussion and investigation by learners into this relationship that does not apply to group 1.

The words in group 3 represent a word family. 'Vehicle' is the main word, while the others are like sub-words indicating different examples of 'vehicle'. Word families are good ways for learners to record new words because they use meaning to make connections. This leads to a stronger memory for the words.

In group 4, the words are related by formality. They have a similar meaning but 'whacky' is much more informal. The over-use of informal vocabulary can be a feature of learners' English and awareness of formal/informal alternatives can expand their vocabulary.

Working with words

Based on the sections above, a focus on meaning when dealing with new words would seem advisable. Some suggestions for a general approach to dealing with words and phrases are now given and then a specific example from a health and social care course is used to provide more ideas.

Embedding ideas

✔ Avoid saying to learners that 'word x' *is the same as* 'word y'. Explore and encourage learners to explore the differences between words. (Is it 'more than', is it 'more formal', etc.)

✔ Have learners place a list of words from your subject area into groups by meaning. By deciding which words to group together, they will discuss a range of meanings and will also discuss and engage with the words. Putting the words on cards makes this a more kinaesthetic activity.

✔ Matching tasks with words – word and definition, word and opposite, word and picture, etc.

✔ *Pelmanism* – This is an extension of matching tasks. The words are printed on cards and turned over. In a memory game, learners turn over cards with words/phrases and find pairs. Through repeated turnings, learners reinforce their understanding of words and increase their visual exposure, which can help spelling.

✔ Show degrees of words on a *cline* or ladder or ask learners to decide how they would be distributed. For example, reorder *filthy, messy, dirty, disgusting* in increasing order of severity. The discussion of which is 'more' can help learners remember the range of words and enhance their use of a variety of terms in their work.

✔ Encourage learners to record new words in a way that relates to meaning. For example, under a topic heading, with opposites or related words.

✔ Use ideas from common word games: learners have to draw a word/mime a word/give similar words to get their team to say the word.

Embedding example

Learners on a health and social care course used the following text as part of their work on charities. The teacher felt that the key words given at the end of the text would be useful to the learners for future work with the topic.

> *Charities are non-profit organizations that benefit the public in some way. In order to qualify to be a charity, an organization has to carry*

out charitable activities, which are quite tightly defined by law. Not all voluntary and non-profit organizations are charities. Unless they are very small, with an income of less than £5,000 a year, charities have to be registered and most register with the Charity Commission.

Charities generate a lot of money by means other than donations. Knowing this is important in appreciating what kind of organizations they are. The common image of amateurish organizations doing their best on a shoestring budget doesn't match the reality of many charities today, or the importance of the work they do.

Key words: *non-profit, voluntary, income, donation, amateurish, shoestring budget*

Embedding ideas

✔ Teacher gives out the words before the text and uses them as a prediction activity for learners to work out the content of the text. (See Chapter 3 on reading)

✔ Learners have to group the words into words connected with *money* and words connected with *work* and justify why they have put them in each group.

✔ Learners are given a word and tasked with finding as many other words that can be used with it as possible. For example, *amateurish production, voluntary redundancy*.

✔ Learners create pelmanism activity for their peers by making pairs with these words and their opposites.

✔ Teacher writes multiple pairs of words on cards to look like dominos. One learner begins a narration on the topic of 'charities'. The next learner has to add their card to either end of the word and continues the narration in a coherent manner.

✔ Each learner in a group is given a word. They have to describe the word/ use words connected to their word without saying the word itself. The rest of the group have to guess the word. For example, for 'donation' – money, gift, giving, reward, altruistic, etc.

Spelling

As mentioned above, part of the accuracy of writing words is getting their spelling correct. Difficulties in spelling can arise from the multiple origins of English words as discussed in Chapter 2, and the lack of correspondence between the way we say words and the way we spell them. For example, the sound under-lined in the words below is the same, but the spelling is very different.

m<u>ee</u>t   m<u>ea</u>t   rec<u>ei</u>ve   bel<u>ie</u>ve   k<u>ey</u>

Different strategies exist to help learners with their spelling. Learners may have a preference for certain strategies. Some may wish to rely more on sound-ing out words, making a link between the sound and the spelling, although as highlighted in the examples above, this can be deceptive. Others may want to use a set of 'rules', while others will try to 'see' the word and remember the spell-ing visually. No one strategy will suit everybody, so encouraging learners to use a range of strategies will help them find the one that suits them.

Embedding tips for spelling

✔ Marking written work helps learners to recognize common spelling errors they make and to focus on these.
✔ Use quizzes to address common spelling errors of the group in relation to key subject words.
✔ Present key words with missing letters as a puzzle (e.g. v _ l _ nta _ y = voluntary) to enhance learners' visual memory of words.
✔ Have some focus on root words and parts that are added on (before *pre-fix* or after *suffix*) to change the word and sometimes the spelling. Exam-ple: *voluntary – involuntary, voluntarily*. There are patterns that learners can recognize, such as 'y' changes to 'ily'.
• Activities such as pelmanism and word games provide learners with repeated exposure to the visual representation of words and can there-fore help in remembering spelling.

Conclusion: language is interesting!

Words and sentences are the building blocks of our spoken and written lan-guage and using them to create meaning is an activity that has rules. When we break these rules, we make a mistake. As teachers, we should encourage our learners to avoid mistakes, particularly in their written English, as this is likely to impact on how successful they are at communicating.

However, a sole focus on accuracy and errors can be demotivating for learners, especially if they lack confidence in their English and have not been successful in using English in the past. Pointing out continuously what is wrong with their English is unlikely to lead to continuing development.

In this chapter, we have looked at some of the more engaging features of English language and approaches that can be used to make language *use* and also *accuracy* interesting for learners. If learners (and teachers) can be enthused about language, they are more likely to invest in improvement that can be sustained long after they finish their course.

Reflective Task – Answers

1. Could you confirm who you had arranged to meet today?
In the second part of the sentence, the subject is 'you' and the object is 'who'. The grammatically correct object pronoun is 'whom'. So the sentence should be: **Can you confirm whom you had arranged to meet today?**

2. The bad weather meant that there were less people than expected at the event.
'People' is a noun that you can count (one person, two people, etc.). Therefore, it must be used with 'fewer'. The correct sentence is: **The bad weather meant that there were fewer people than expected at the event.**

3. We missed you at the party, where was you?
The form of the verb 'to be' when used with 'you' is 'were'. 'Was' is only used with 'I', 'he', 'she' or 'it'. The correct sentence is: **We missed you at the party, where were you?**

4. The economic downturn continues to effect purchasing power.
The verb is spelled 'affect', the noun is spelled 'effect'. In this sentence, the verb ought to be used. The correct sentence is: **The economic downturn continues to affect purchasing power.**

5. Several student's handed in their work late.
The 's' at the end of 'student' is simply used to make it plural. There is no use of the possessive and therefore no apostrophe. The correct sentence is: **Several students handed in their work late.**

6. He fractured a cup.
Although 'fractured' has a similar meaning to 'broke', it is not used with 'cup'; it is normally associated with bones. The correct sentence is: **He broke/ cracked a cup.**

Further reading

If you are interested in the debate about the importance of accuracy and the recognition of language change, two excellent books to consult (offering opposing views) are:

Crystal, D. (2006) *The Fight for English: How Language Pundits Ate, Shot and Left*. Oxford: Oxford University Press.
Truss, L. (2009) *Eats, Shoots and Leaves*. London: Fourth Estate.

Grammar/spelling reference books

Crystal, D. (2004) *Rediscover Grammar*. Oxford: Oxford University Press.

Crystal, D. (2013) *Spell It Out: The Singular Story of English Spelling*. Oxford: Oxford University Press.

Truss, L. (2009) *Eats, Shoots and Leaves*. London: Fourth Estate.

Grammar references particularly useful for ESOL learners

Murphy, R. (2002) *English Grammar in Use*. Cambridge: Cambridge University Press. Easy for learners to self-access.

Swan, M. (2005) *Practical English Usage* (3rd edn.). Oxford: Oxford University Press. Probably more useful for teachers.

Other reading

Swan, M. and Smith, B (2001) *Learner English: A Teacher's Guide to Interference and Other Problems*. Cambridge: Cambridge University Press. Highlights specific language problems, including grammar, for learners with a specific first language. In other words, the typical errors you would expect to find a learner with a specific first language makes.

Thornbury, S. (1997) *About Language*. Cambridge: Cambridge University Press. A very accessible book if you are interested in finding out more about language in general. The first half is a series of discovery tasks and the second half a key with explanations.

6 Phonology and specific issues for speakers of English as a second language

Reflective Task

1. Has your own accent changed during your life? If yes, what reasons might there be for this change?
2. Have you ever had your pronunciation corrected? If so, how did you feel?
3. When learning another language, was pronunciation important for you? Why? Why not?

See the end of the chapter for some discussion on these questions.

What do we mean by 'pronunciation'?

The reflective task above is intended to get you to think about the way you speak and this is what we mean by pronunciation. It encompasses the different ways that people say sounds, words and sentences as a result of a number of factors. The different ways people speak reflect the accents of their *variety* of English.

One of the main deciders of the variety of English you speak is the place you grew up. Thus many varieties are geographical. Examples of major varieties include American, British and Australian English. But even within relatively small areas of the UK, there are many regional varieties.

Another deciding factor can be the social group with which you associate. In the UK, social groups are often connected to the idea of social class. Some will identify a *posh* or *upper-class* accent as being distinct from a *middle-* or *working-class* accent. Your accent may also be connected to the social group related to your work rather than a social class.

Language variety is more wide-reaching than pronunciation and includes choice of vocabulary and grammar. This is most obvious in age-related varieties whereby parents and their children use very different terms to refer to the same things and events. However, their pronunciation of words is likely to be very similar.

There is no right or wrong variety of English, but there are varieties that may be highly valued in certain situations. If you move out of your geographical area, you may feel that your accent is less valued than the accent of the area you have moved to. In the UK, positive values are sometimes placed on accents associated with the south-east of England. This may, however, depend on the group you are communicating with.

Any change in our pronunciation is thus likely to be due to the desire to be valued and to fit in with the group we are with. One example of this is our 'phone voice', the way of speaking we adopt when we speak formally to someone we do not know on the phone. This new accent is likely to have an element of the accent we perceive as more correct or acceptable.

Since there is no right or wrong variety of English, it would not be good practice in our classroom to correct our learners' pronunciation if they are native speakers. However, it is useful to raise their awareness of some of the issues discussed so far, particularly the idea of accents that are valued. This will make them more cognizant of their own variety, the impact of their pronunciation on others, and the inappropriateness of making judgements about others based on their accent.

Embedding ideas

In order to raise awareness of pronunciation issues with learners who are native speakers of English, you could undertake some of the following as part of your classroom practice.

✓ Where learners undertake interviews, ask them to focus on the different accents of the people they interview, particularly individual words related to your vocational context. Discuss this as a *difference*, not better or worse ways of saying things.

✓ Use speakers with different varieties of English when selecting any audio materials such as video. Discuss the different accents, again focusing on different varieties.

✓ Play examples of different accents and relate this to situations in your vocational context. For example, who would you trust most to sell you a product, who do you think is telling the truth, who has the most knowledge. Draw out and critique some of the values placed on accents, including being associated with honesty, intelligence, etc.

Pronunciation and ESOL learners

For learners who have English as a second language, their first language is likely to affect the way they speak English. They will have an accent that is not characteristic of a variety of English. In addition, they may pronounce words in ways that interfere with the listener's understanding. They may therefore have difficulty making themselves understood when speaking to others.

For such learners, it is just as important to address accuracy in pronunciation as to address grammatical accuracy in writing. Many teachers are hesitant about doing this, possibly because it relates to the issues raised above about certain accents having value and the feeling that we might be devaluing what a learner says if we correct their pronunciation. However, the effectiveness of speaking depends on a mainly accurate pronunciation, perhaps even more so than accuracy of grammar. We are not helping ESOL learners by not providing some feedback on their pronunciation.

What ESOL leaners find difficult

Sounds

There are fixed sounds or *phonemes* that are associated with the English language. There are 26 letters in the English alphabet, but there are 44 sounds that are characteristic of English. Twenty-four of these are consonant sounds: the sounds we associate with the letters p, t, th, v, etc. The other 20 are vowel sounds: the sounds we associate with the letters a, e, i, o and u, and combinations of these letters. A full illustration of these sounds is given by the *phonemic alphabet*, which is a set of symbols used to represent sounds. The phonemic alphabet is used in dictionaries to show how a word is pronounced. It is not necessary for you to know the phonemic alphabet, but some of your ESOL learners may be very familiar with it and use it to help them with the pronunciation of sounds. A couple of examples are given below for illustration purposes (Tables 6.1 and 6.2). All the symbols in the phonemic alphabet are written between two slash marks '/ /' to show that they are not real letters. The corresponding sound in the example words is underlined.

Table 6.1 Consonant sounds

Phonemic symbol	Example
/ p /	Petal, apartment, app
/ ð /	The, then, other
/ ʃ /	Shower, shun, information
/ v /	Very, obvious, love

Table 6.2 Vowel sounds

Phonemic symbol	Example
/ iː /	S<u>ee</u>, rel<u>ea</u>se, m<u>ea</u>t
/ æ /	C<u>a</u>t, s<u>a</u>nd, l<u>a</u>nguage
/ aI /	Cr<u>y</u>, l<u>ie</u>, dec<u>i</u>de
/ e /	L<u>e</u>t, r<u>e</u>nt, b<u>e</u>tter

Not all the sounds of English are used in other languages, and some sounds that are different in English are not distinct in other languages. For example, the sounds 'l' and 'r' are not distinct in Japanese, so learners whose first language is Japanese will have difficulty hearing the difference and choosing the right sound to say. The sound 'th' does not exist in French or German and so speakers of those languages will have to learn to say this sound.

There is also much potential for confusion between sounds and spelling. As may be clear from the examples in the tables above, this is most evident with vowel sounds. The examples show that one sound can be realized in different spellings. The lack of correspondence between sounds and letters is also confusing to native speakers, as outlined in Chapter 5, because learners will want to write the same letter for the same sound they hear. However, it is doubly confusing for ESOL learners, who will also want to say a new word they come across as it is spelled. This impacts on their speaking as well as their writing.

Word stress

In English, for words that are made up of more than one syllable, a stress is placed on one or more of the syllables. This stress sounds like an emphasis being placed on one or more parts of the word. Say the following words out loud as naturally as you can:

information   Saturday   upset

As you say them, it should be clear that one syllable is 'stronger' than the others. The stronger syllable is underlined in the words below. As you can see, the stress can be at the beginning, in the middle or at the end of words.

infor<u>ma</u>tion   <u>Sat</u>urday   up<u>set</u>

Getting this stress pattern right is part of making the word understandable to others. It also impacts on the sounds within the word. Say the following words out loud and notice what happens to the sound of the syllable that is written 'for'.

inform   information   informative

In the first and third word, the syllable 'for' is pronounced in a similar way. In the second word, because the stress has moved to the syllable 'ma', the pronunciation of 'for' is quite different. These changes are difficult for ESOL learners to recognize when they see the word in its written form.

Not all languages have this way of placing stress on certain syllables in a word. Other languages, such as French, stress all syllables more equally and therefore the pronunciation of different parts of words does not change. For learners whose first language is similar to the way French is stressed, the changing patterns in English are very challenging. They may sound 'robotic' when they speak or say words with a stress pattern that makes them difficult to understand.

Embedding ideas for pronunciation work with ESOL learners

✓ **Idea 1**
Don't ignore or be embarrassed about addressing pronunciation! Accurate pronunciation is as fundamental to the learners' communication as correct grammar or spelling. It is, of course, important to deal with pronunciation in a sensitive way, but not dealing with it will be detrimental to the learners' progress.

✓ **Idea 2**
Identify important subject words that learners need and ensure you model them clearly and ask learners to repeat them. You need to say new words a couple of times and encourage learners to say them aloud to check they have got the correct pronunciation.

With a group of ESOL learners, this is not a problem. With a mixed group, you may have to do some individual work because asking learners to repeat words out loud may be embarrassing. There is no substitute for hearing a word, noticing the sound and trying to say it. There is a psychomotor element to pronunciation that benefits from simple repetition.

✓ **Idea 3**
For longer words that learners find difficult to pronounce, break the word up from the end. This helps to maintain the sound relationships and stress patterns within the word. For example, if a learner has difficulty with the word 'communication', you could break it down in the following stages, model each one and ask the learner to repeat:

- tion

- cation

- munication

- communication

✓ **Idea 4**

Include pronunciation errors in your formative feedback on speaking activities. As you listen to learners, remain tuned in to pronunciation errors as well as grammar or content issues. In feedback, highlight words that have been mispronounced and encourage learners to self- and peer-correct.

✓ **Idea 5**

Remain aware and make use of the sound element in spelling. Learner error may be due to a lack of sound awareness and this may suggest that you use sound-based strategies to help with spelling.

One strategy is to focus on different sounds with different spellings – for example, beat – bit – bet – bat – but. In pairs, learners take it in turns to say them while their partner points to the one they hear.

Another strategy is to look at words with the same sound but different spelling – meat, meet – and draw attention to the fact that English letters do not always have a correspondence to the way they are pronounced.

Embedding example: gas exchange

On the physiology module of a sports science course, the teacher is introducing the main functions of different organs of the body. Below is a short extract from the teacher's notes for the session on the functions of the lung.

> *The primary function of the lung is gas exchange. There are other functions of the lung. For example, it filters material from the blood, it has metabolic functions as well as acting as a reservoir for blood. But by far its most important function is gas exchange. It's therefore important to look at what happens directly at the blood-gas barrier where the diffusive gas exchange occurs.*

Consider what key words the teacher would want to focus on for the ESOL learners in the group. What would be the important things to highlight about the pronunciation of these words? See the end of the chapter for some suggestions.

Pronunciation: sentence and text

So far, we have considered mainly the pronunciation of sounds and words. However, your learners will need to speak in sentences and longer stretches, which we call 'spoken text'. Within these speaking activities, it is important to get individual sounds as comprehensible as possible for those listening, but there are other features of spoken English that can also be challenging for learners with English as a second language.

Sentence stress

Within a sentence, we place more stress on certain words. In general, it is the important words or 'content words' that are stressed. Say the sentence that follows out loud as naturally as possible:

A return to London please.

The important or content words in the sentence are those that will ensure the listener understands the purpose of what you say. In this sentence, the words 'return' and 'London' are the most important. You may also have given some emphasis to the 'please', but it is unlikely that you have stressed either 'a' or 'to'. Grammatical words are not usually stressed in sentences. Your example probably ended up something like this:

A **return** to **London** please.

Another important feature of English is that the unstressed words ('a' and 'to' in this sentence) seem to shrink and are hardly audible. This is a natural feature of English and it is important that we do not encourage learners to 'over-pronounce' these words. For example:

Eh return **too** London please.

You may be tempted to think that this is a correct pronunciation, but in fact it is unnatural and will lead learners to be less able to manage the articulation of sentences.

Intonation

Intonation is the word used to describe the way the pitch or tone of your voice goes up and down as you speak. It plays an important part in creating meaning in English. Take the word 'really' and say it a number of times in different contexts, such as:

Really

- To show excitement at new information
- To show disappointment
- To show disbelief
- To show disapproval
- To show disinterest

You will notice that even within this one word your voice goes up and down to indicate your feelings about the situation. It is the same for sentences and longer stretches of spoken text. One of the features of English is that it has a wider *range* of pitch than many other languages. This means that the difference between the lowest and highest pitch a speaker uses is quite pronounced.

Learners whose first language is not English may encounter some difficulty with intonation. When listening to native speakers, they may not be able to decipher the intended meaning and so may not pick up that the speaker is indicating disapproval, sarcasm, excitement, etc. By focusing on the words only, they may not understand the full extent of what is being said to them.

A second issue is an inability to replicate English intonation when speaking, which may result in an unintended meaning being communicated. For example, learners whose pitch does not vary greatly may be perceived as being disinterested, as their speech will resemble the way you said 'really' above to indicate disinterest. The impact is even greater if learners are communicating in a context with few other indicators, such as facial expression, when on the phone for example.

Some learners may also feel that the change in pitch in English is somewhat comical or embarrassing and may not wish to replicate it. This is something to discuss with your learners in terms of their speaking choices and the impact they want to have on the listener.

Embedding ideas for sentence stress and intonation

✓ Model sentences naturally. Avoid overstressing words even when you want to correct something a learner has said. If you need to focus on a word that is mispronounced, make sure you repeat the whole sentence afterwards more naturally.

✓ Encourage learners to highlight important/content words when they are preparing presentations so that these are more likely to be the words they stress.

✓ When watching videos of groups interacting, prepare some questions on the meaning that is communicated by intonation. For example, is person X happy/afraid/doubtful, etc. Try to encourage learners to identify the meaning that comes from pitch and tone rather than words. This is a useful skill for all learners to work with as preparation for social interactions, but is particularly important for ESOL learners.

✓ Be cognizant of your own and other learners' reaction to speakers who are not fully aware of the impact of intonation. Avoid drawing conclusions as to the learner's attitude or reaction based on the fact that what they say may sound rather 'flat', disinterested or even aggressive. This may in no way reflect the speaker's intentions.

Working with different spoken genres

It is likely that you will ask your learners to engage in different spoken genres in class – for example, discussion, debate, presentation, negotiation. All of these will probably be familiar to your learners, but some of the speaking skills needed may be very challenging for any ESOL learners.

One issue that can be particularly difficult is the idea of 'turn-taking' or 'interrupting'. In spoken activities, we usually hand over the conversation at different stages or indicate that we would now like to say something in a fairly polite manner. The intonation and language for doing this is quite specific and can be challenging if English is not your first language.

Embedding ideas for speaking activities

✓ As with writing, it is a good idea to show learners examples of the spoken genre as a model. If you are preparing for a discussion, show them an example of a discussion (positive or negative) and pose questions as to how the participants were successful (or not) in their roles. A specific focus on language used to interrupt or to hand over to others will be useful.

✓ **Rehearsal** – It is very important to recognize the additional preparation time that may be needed by ESOL learners to prepare for a speaking activity. They may need time in pairs or groups to rehearse what they are going to say. For example, in a whole-class question-and-answer review, having a five-minute opportunity for learners to work in pairs and groups to review without the exposure to whole-class interaction may be very beneficial to ESOL learners, and possibly to other learners as well.

Embedding example

Below is a transcript of the verbal instructions given by a teacher of a health and social studies class to set up a discussion activity. About half the class are learners who have English as a second language. What could the teacher have done to embed the development of spoken language?

> *Today we're going to look at some of the issues around the care of the elderly. We did some work on this yesterday. I want you to work in groups of four. Two of you will be in favour of the statement and two will be against. You will take turns to present your arguments. Have a think for a minute and then I'll say 'start'. The statement is:*
>
> *'The care of the elderly is the responsibility of the family, not the state'. OK, go.*

Embedding example – suggestions

✔ **Review of key words** – if the topic has already been discussed, then it would be easy to simply ask the class for some of these. The words can then be modelled through learner suggestion. Even the words 'responsible'/'responsibility' can pose pronunciation problems. In preparation for the lesson, the teacher could select some key words and identify potential pronunciation difficulties for learners.

✔ **The genre** – the activity is set up as a debate where learners must take a position that they may not even agree with. This may be something unfamiliar to learners and needs to be discussed beforehand. There also needs to be agreement as to the expectations of the interaction. Are learners expected to speak at length and then have their arguments refuted or are they expected to respond to each individual point made?

✔ **Rehearsal time** – learners need time to plan what they will say. ESOL learners may need to plan in more detail, including making notes on the specific language they will use. A suggestion would be to put all the 'in favour' learners together to prepare and then regroup them with pairs of the 'against' learners to engage in the discussion.

The instructions of the teacher given above are an example of an activity that seems on the surface to be embedding speaking skills because the learners are engaging in speaking. However, it is likely that learners will leave the lesson no more adept at discussion/debate than when they arrived.

Reflective task – discussion

1. Has your own accent changed during your life?

If yes, what reasons are there for this change? You may decide that your 'accent' changes over a day – depending on the situations you find yourself speaking in. But over your lifetime, you may have moved and developed a particular regional accent or you may have adopted the accent of groups to which you belonged. In each case, it is likely that your accent changed to fit in or assimilate in some way with others.

2. Have you ever had your pronunciation corrected? If so, how did you feel?

It is possible that you have had your accent corrected because it was different to that of the person who 'corrected' you. The person who corrected you will no doubt have felt that there accent was of a correct standard and that they were advising you on a more accurate way to say something. Correction of pronunciation is likely to be taken quite personally because it addresses a very personal area – the way we speak and communicate.

3. When learning another language, was pronunciation important for you? Why? Why not?

If you have learned another language, you will be aware that some pronunciation is quite difficult and challenging and that you need a lot of practice in this area. For some people, accurate pronunciation is not that important as long as the main message is communicated.

Embedding example: gas exchange – suggestions

The primary function of the lung is gas exchange. There are other functions of the lung. For example, it filters material from the blood, it has metabolic functions as well as acting as a reservoir for blood. But by far its most important function is gas exchange. It's therefore important to look at what happens directly at the blood-gas barrier where the diffusive gas exchange occurs.

It would be good for the teacher to focus on some of the subject content words:

- gas exchange
- filters
- metabolic
- diffusive

Gas exchange – difficult relationship between the letters 'exch' and the sound. The 'ng' sound can also be difficult. Stress is on the second syllable of 'exchange', so the first syllable is very 'small'.

Filters – the stress is on the first syllable. No real sound issues.

Metabolic – the stress is on 'bol'. The teacher might highlight that in words that end in '-ic', the stress is usually on the syllable before '-ic'.

Diffusive – there is a long 'u' sound in the middle where the main stress is. The spelling of 'sive' suggests that the 'i' is pronounced as letter 'i', but this is not the case.

Conclusion

In this chapter we have looked at some of the challenges of developing learners' speaking skills for both native speakers of English and those who have English as a second language. The sensitivities around addressing pronunciation and the way people speak can sometimes discourage us from a deliberate focus on speaking and providing feedback. However, for ESOL students, improvements in the way they pronounce sounds, words and sentences contribute significantly to their speaking skills and their confidence.

In most lessons, learners speak and contribute at length. Simply allowing them space to speak does not necessarily mean that you are developing their speaking skills. Hopefully this chapter has given you some ideas for a more deliberate focus on speaking and will support your work with all learners.

Part 2
Supporting Maths in Post-14 Education and Training

7   Introduction to maths

Reflective Task

Look at the following lesson ideas and think about the maths involved.

- Learners in a performing arts lesson are working in groups of four to create a dance routine based on shape and symmetry. Routines need to be four minutes long and contain at least two movement repeats.
- A sport science lesson is focusing on health and safety issues at the local sport centre. One area they need to consider is the water quality in the swimming pool.
- Learners on an equine management course are looking at the different nutritional requirements of a foal and a lactating mare.

Now think about your own teaching and begin to identify some of the opportunities that arise for including maths in your specialist area.

Based on the reflective task above, you may have identified that maths is an important part of your subject and that you use it regularly within your teaching. Some subject areas contain more opportunities to involve maths than others. If you found it difficult to identify the maths within your teaching, some of your initial thoughts may be reflected in the following typical responses from new (and some not so new) teachers:

Maths isn't relevant in my subject specialism.
I don't know what maths I am expected to include.
I'm anxious about/not confident with maths myself, so how can I be expected to teach it?
Aren't there specialist teachers who teach maths?

It can be helpful to discuss concerns with maths with other teachers, in order to appreciate that others may well have similar concerns.

Opportunities to include maths in your teaching

> ### Task 7.1
>
> List some of the topics in your specialist area that will involve learners using maths.
>
> Focus on one of the topics you have listed and think about planning an activity that will help to develop your learners' maths skills. As with planning any activity, it will be important to consider the following:
>
> a) The prior knowledge that learners need in order to access and successfully achieve the activity.
> b) A suitable extension activity.

Example 1

The list of a teacher of art might include the use of scale in enlarging and reducing pictures, design work that uses two- and three-dimensional shapes, and the accurate use of measurement for display purposes.

a) Focusing on the prior knowledge required to enlarge a design, learners will need to be familiar with scale and ratio, which in turn depends on multiplication and division skills.
b) A suitable extension activity might include enlarging a design in three-dimensional space.

Example 2

A teacher of hospitality and catering might list the use of time, weight, ratio and proportion and fractions.

a) Focusing on the prior knowledge required to increase or decrease a quantity of ingredients to cater for a given number of people, learners will need to be familiar with ratio and proportion, which relies on multiplication and division skills. They also need to be aware of the common units of measure and the associated conversion factors, so they are able to convert between grams and kilograms.
b) A suitable extension task could include more complex ratios based on different numbers of customers.

There are some useful publications available that can help guide your choice of activity and level of topic. In 2000, the Department for Education and Skills (DfES) and the Qualifications and Curriculum Authority (QCA) published the first national standards for adult literacy and numeracy. The standards provide a set of skills statements with guidance and examples at each level, outlining the underpinning knowledge and understanding that act as building blocks for functional skills. The standards for adult numeracy formed the basis of the Adult Numeracy Core Curriculum (ANCC), published by the Basic Skills Agency in 2001. The publication is no longer in print, but a PDF copy and an updated and widely extended version are both available on the Excellence Gateway website.

The ANCC and the 2011 Ofqual Functional Skills Criteria for Mathematics are helpful documents for providing an indication of the coverage and the type of skills that learners can be expected to use, from Entry Level 1 to Level 2.

It is important to be aware of the progression levels of different topics, to help ensure that any planned maths tasks provide an appropriate level of challenge. Learners tend to lose focus more quickly with activities that are either too easy or too challenging. Tasks that are too complex may result in disengagement and create additional anxiety for some learners. It is equally important to be aware that other factors influence the actual or perceived level of difficulty, including a learner's familiarity with a topic and its relevance to their everyday life.

The functional skills coverage for maths topics between Entry Level 1 and Level 2 (Ofqual, 2011) is shown in Table 7.1.

Now look back at one of the activities you devised for Task 7.1.

- Use the functional skills coverage in Table 7.1 to decide whether the activity you selected was suitable for the level at which your learners are working.
- Does your extension activity advance the skill towards the next level, or extend the skill to incorporate additional skills at the same level?

Learners come to class with different prior experiences of learning maths. They will have attended different schools and will have developed different attitudes towards learning maths. Most people have a spiky profile of skills, which means there are some areas of maths that they are better at and more confident with than others. This can result in learners being on two or more levels for different skills. For example, someone may be very poor at reading timetables, but very good at managing their own money. It is important to focus on learners' areas of strength, as reinforcing what they can already do helps to build confidence and can gradually be extended to help them develop new skills.

Table 7.1 Functional skills coverage for mathematics

Entry Level 1	Entry Level 2	Entry Level 3
Understand and use numbers with one significant figure in practical contexts	Understand and use whole numbers with up to two significant figures	Add and subtract using three-digit numbers
Describe the properties of size and measure, including length, width, height and weight, and make simple comparisons	Understand and use addition/subtraction in practical situations	Solve practical problems involving multiplication and division by 2, 3, 4, 5 and 10
Describe position	Use doubling and halving in practical situations	Round to the nearest 10 or 100
Recognize and select coins and notes	Recognize and use familiar measures, including time and money	Understand and use simple fractions
Recognize and name common 2D and 3D shapes	Recognize sequences of numbers, including odd and even numbers	Understand, estimate, measure and compare length, capacity, weight and temperature
Sort and classify objects practically using a single criterion	Use simple scales and measure to the nearest labelled division	Understand decimals to two decimal places in practical contexts
	Know properties of simple 2D and 3D shapes	Recognize and describe number patterns
	Extract information from simple lists	Complete simple calculations involving money and measures
		Recognize and name simple 2D and 3D shapes and their properties
		Use metric units in everyday situations
		Extract, use and compare information from lists, tables, simple charts and simple graphs

(continued)

Table 7.1 Functional skills coverage for mathematics (*Continued*)

Level 1	Level 2
Understand and use whole numbers and understand negative numbers in practical contexts	Understand and use positive and negative numbers of any size in practical contexts
Add, subtract, multiply and divide whole numbers using a range of strategies	Carry out calculations with numbers of any size in practical contexts, to a given number of decimal places
Understand and use equivalences between common fractions, decimals and percentages	Understand, use and calculate ratio and proportion, including problems involving scale
Add and subtract decimals up to two decimal places	Understand and use equivalences between fractions, decimals and percentages
Solve simple problems involving ratio, where one number is a multiple of the other	Understand and use simple formulae and equations involving one or two operations
Use simple formulae expressed in words for one- or two-step operations	Recognize and use 2D representations of 3D objects
Solve problems requiring calculation, with common measures, including money, time, length, weight, capacity and temperature	Find area, perimeter and volume of common shapes
	Use, convert and calculate using metric and, where appropriate, imperial measures
Convert units of measure in the same system	Collect and represent discrete and continuous data, using information and communication technology (ICT) where appropriate
Work out areas and perimeters in practical situations	
Construct geometric diagrams, models and shapes	Use and interpret statistical measures, tables and diagrams, for discrete and continuous data, using information and communication technology (ICT) where appropriate
Extract and interpret information from tables, diagrams, charts and graphs	
Collect and record discrete data and organize and represent information in different ways	Use statistical methods to investigate situations
Find mean and range	Use probability to assess the likelihood of an outcome
Use data to assess the likelihood of an outcome	

Source: Adapted from Ofqual (2011). Contains public sector information licensed under the Open Government Licence v3.0.

It is not intended that vocational teachers work systematically through each skill with their learners, but rather that teachers are aware of the way different skills can be developed and what might be expected at each level.

What do you need to do?

This section of the chapter is intended to encourage you to consider some of the terminology that was introduced in Chapter 1 and to begin to think about what the different terms mean with regard to including maths in your own teaching.

Embed

Fully embedding maths in a learning programme should mean that a learner is able to achieve two qualifications within the one programme, the vocational qualification and a maths qualification. For this to be successful, the programme would need to be carefully planned and taught by a specialist vocational teacher working with a maths teacher to ensure the learning outcome for both qualifications is achieved. The vocational teacher is a specialist in his or her own field; they are likely to be comfortable with the maths that is involved in their subject, but may not have the breadth of skills required of a maths teacher. Similarly, the maths teacher knows the maths, but is unlikely to be familiar with the content of every vocational programme, so may not recognize some of the opportunities that arise to make the maths more meaningful to learners.

With the increased national focus on raising attainment in maths, there is a growing expectation for all teachers in the learning and skills sector to embed maths (and English) in their teaching. This expectation can lead to teachers feeling uncertain or even anxious about what maths to include and how it should be effectively embedded.

Using embedded approaches doesn't mean that vocational teachers need to become maths and English teachers. It means that they need to be aware of the opportunities that arise naturally in their programmes for reinforcing and developing maths skills, and to plan lessons that enable learners to consolidate and develop their personal maths skills in a practical and realistic setting. The opportunities need to be built in, rather than bolted on to the current learning programme.

Contextualize

Learners who enrol on vocational programmes of study are generally more interested in the vocational area than in developing their maths skills. It makes sense therefore to use scenarios set within the vocational context to help motivate learners and to encourage them to re-engage with some key mathematical concepts. Problem-solving scenarios that are set in a vocational context can be used to help reinforce and consolidate understanding of previously learned skills, or they can be used to introduce new maths skills. It is important that the scenario used is meaningful to the learner and relevant to the vocational or life context. A household budgeting task may be relevant for a group of adult learners who are managing their own budgets, but council tax and electricity bills hold less interest for a 16-year-old who still lives at home.

Contextualizing tasks so they are relevant to learners' interests can be a good starting point for encouraging learners to develop more positive attitudes towards maths. However, at some stage it will be important for your learners to work towards being able to solve problems in different contexts. Functional Skills exams questions are contextualized, but the exam papers are designed for learners from a range of vocational areas and so the questions present a range of different work and life situations. Maths GCSE papers also include questions that are set in context and are designed to assess a learner's functional application of mathematics. Therefore, when your learners are secure with maths concepts in a familiar context, it will be good practice to check whether they are able to transfer their understanding to less familiar contexts, to help prepare them for exams.

Although planning scenarios that involve learners in using ratio in your own vocational area may be quite straightforward, you may find it helpful to collaborate with other vocational or specialist tutors for authentic ideas that will enable your learners to apply ratio in other situations, so that they are ultimately able to transfer their understanding of ratio beyond their own vocational context.

Use every opportunity

This approach should be adopted and developed throughout your planning, teaching and assessment of learning. During planning, actively consider where maths opportunities arise. In the classroom, begin to recognize and utilize opportunities as they arise, using what the learners know and understand to reinforce and develop their mathematical thinking. Trainee teachers and new teachers are unlikely to recognize every opportunity, but when situations arise while you are teaching, note them down as part of your lesson evaluation and think about how you can incorporate them into future teaching. Share ideas and strategies with colleagues so you develop your repertoire of including maths wherever you can.

Embedding reminders

Whether embedding, contextualizing or just using every opportunity, it is important:

✓ To incorporate any maths in a relevant and meaningful way.
✓ For vocational and maths teachers to work together to identify and maximize the opportunities for incorporating maths in vocational contexts.

Other opportunities can arise during your working day for reinforcing and developing your learners' maths skills. Personal tutors have responsibility for monitoring their tutees' overall progress and well-being. This will involve encouraging your learners to develop wider skills in preparation for life and work, and may include providing guidance in some aspects of time management and budgeting.

Using maths every day

Task 7.2

a)   Think about the maths skills you have used in the past 24 hours.
b)   Make a list of all the activities where you used some form of maths.

Everybody's list will be different, but it is likely that you have included some aspect of using time, money, and reading and interpreting information from charts or tables. Some of the activities may have demanded an accurate calculation, whereas for others an estimate would have been sufficient. It is also likely that you carried out some of these activities without thinking about the maths. You started with a purpose and devised a strategy that hopefully enabled you to work out what you needed.

Task 7.2 should highlight that many maths topics are interdependent. The headings that I have chosen for the following three maths chapters are based on the Adult Numeracy Core Curriculum areas of (1) Number, (2) Measure, Shape and Space, and (3) Data Handling. However, this is largely a matter of convenience and it should be remembered that prior learning requirements often cross these topic boundaries. For example, measuring a room in order to fit new skirting board or weighing ingredients for dinner would require an understanding of metric units of length and weight. These skills would be included in the measure, shape and space category, but are clearly underpinned by knowledge of number.

To develop good study skills, learners in any curriculum area will need to be able to organize their time, prioritize tasks and meet deadlines.

Task 7.3

Look at a timetable for one of the classes you teach and think about:

a) How you can encourage learners to engage with their timetable and begin to take responsibility for their own learning.
b) The skills they need in order to use their timetables effectively to plan and organize their work.

Now decide whether these skills use aspects of number, measure or handling data. You have probably noticed that once again the skills cross the different categories.

Making maths functional

Hopefully you are beginning to appreciate that, unless you are a maths teacher, you are not expected to teach a full maths curriculum to your learners, but rather that you are able to plan suitable ways to introduce and reinforce the maths skills that arise naturally in your subject. It is important that your learners are able to apply their maths skills in practical situations and so become functional in using mathematics.

Learners often view maths as a series of unrelated topics that rely on them memorizing a set of rules. Doing maths is not just about learning a set of procedures – either just for the sake of it, or to apply to problem-solving. It also involves developing an ability to think logically, to plan and organize work systematically, and to be able to interpret and communicate results. These are all important transferable skills that contribute to young people obtaining and maintaining employment.

Functional maths involves problem-solving situations set in a particular context. There are different ways to approach problem-solving tasks and many learners will be familiar with a traditional approach that introduces a maths skill or concept via a teacher demonstration. Typically, the demonstration is followed by the learner practising a number of similar questions, either from a worksheet or a textbook. Once the skill has been practised, learners can then apply the skill in a practical situation that may or may not relate to their vocational context. This approach will work for some learners but others may not appreciate why they are learning the skill and, if they view the approach as too similar to the one they experienced at school, they may become de-motivated and disengage from the activity. There are also likely to be some learners who do not complete the practice examples and so do not get as far as the more interesting questions set in context. In addition, a teaching approach that demonstrates a method followed by practice examples doesn't necessarily encourage learners to transfer their skills to a different context.

An alternative approach is to start with a problem set in context. Problem-solving scenarios can be used to check and consolidate previous learning, but can also be used to introduce new skills. For example, learners could be introduced to a problem that would arise in their vocational area of interest and then try to solve it. The context provides the justification for learning the maths skills. Working in small groups and discussing a problem with others can be a useful way for learners to develop their mathematical reasoning and understanding. Learners are able to share strategies and through discussion with others can test and clarify their ideas. This can help them to develop confidence and begin to recognize when particular strategies can be applied. The teacher's role is to facilitate discussion between the learners and to guide them as they work towards a solution.

Embedding reminder

✔ Don't assume a learner can master a skill in one task and then immediately transfer that skill to another task or context.
✔ Introduce a realistic problem set in a vocational context to encourage learners to consolidate and develop their maths skills.

Collaborative activities may need to be introduced gradually if learners are not familiar with working on problem-solving tasks together. This may involve starting with just a short activity for one part of the lesson, so learners can become accustomed to working together to discuss and share their ideas and maths strategies.

Issues in developing learners' mathematical knowledge

Teachers' confidence in their own maths skills

Lack of familiarity with the contents of a maths curriculum or a lack of confidence with personal maths skills can lead to teachers being reluctant to engage their own learners in mathematical tasks. Teachers may be concerned about creating further confusion for their learners if they show them an alternative method or procedure, and may also think that they need to have all the answers. Examples of different strategies for calculating and suggestions for approaches to managing groups of learners who calculate in different ways are discussed in Chapter 8.

It may be helpful to revisit the list you developed for Task 7.1 and consider which topics you are confident with and which topics you might need to review or perhaps discuss with colleagues. Begin to create a bank of resources that you will be able to use to support and develop your learners' maths skills. Some of the activities in the following three chapters will encourage you to consider different strategies and approaches to teaching and learning maths, and you will be encouraged to think about adapting some of the activities for use with your learners.

Knowing the learners' starting point

Learners on a Level 1 vocational course may have maths skills that range between Entry Level and Level 2. This means that the maths within tasks will need to be differentiated to ensure learners are able to access and succeed at the task on their own level.

It is helpful to have some initial assessment information that provides an indication of your learners' maths levels and starting points. However, as discussed earlier, learners will have spiky profiles and so your own observations and assessment of their participation and confidence will be important factors in determining the way you plan and manage different activities.

Refer to the functional skills levels in Table 7.1 to help ensure you are providing maths tasks that are suitable for your learners and accessible at a range of levels.

Learners' attitudes and emotional responses to learning maths

Many learners in further education have developed negative attitudes towards learning mathematics. Some of the factors associated with a negative attitude include a lack of confidence, limited competence and a failure to see the relevance of the maths.

A useful way to help your learners begin to overcome any barriers and negative emotions about maths is to get them to discuss their thoughts about learning maths, preferably at the beginning of their vocational programme. If learners do have negative attitudes towards maths, they are more likely to feel secure if they are able to discuss their initial thoughts in small groups of three or four. The activity can be quite cathartic and might be usefully followed up with a non-threatening activity that illustrates the role of maths in the vocational area. Learners are often relieved to find others who share similar attitudes. It is also helpful for you to recognize your learners' concerns and to begin to think about how you can continue to encourage and support them in developing their skills and confidence in using mathematics.

Maths anxiety

Some of your learners may have developed such negative emotions towards maths that they feel tense and anxious whenever you attempt to introduce anything related to numbers. They may express their dislike or try to avoid situations that involve them in using maths and may refuse to engage with a task. A build-up of avoiding maths tasks throughout the school years is likely to result in gaps in maths knowledge and reduced levels of competence; this clearly impacts learners' ability to engage in tasks and creates a cycle of avoidance. Others may experience an emotional panic that leads to a block in their ability to process any information. Learners may also have developed a fear of appearing stupid in front of their peers, or of being found out and exposed as the only one who cannot do the maths. These feelings can be a learned response to previous maths learning experiences, and will invariably have a negative impact on learners' levels of confidence. Maths anxiety and a lack of confidence in personal maths skills are not confined to learners, but can also impact the workplace. As the workplace includes the education sector, it is particularly important for teachers to be aware of their own attitudes towards maths so that they do not contribute to reinforcing negative attitudes in their learners.

Key things to work towards include developing a positive relationship with your learners, and encouraging them to discuss and share their feelings about maths and to focus on the maths that is relevant in their vocational area. It is important for learners to experience success and to be able to identify and acknowledge the maths that they are already using.

Use of calculators

A calculator is a tool that we use to help solve practical problems in real life. Skills in using a calculator need to be developed alongside skills that develop mental strategies for problem-solving. Learners can use a calculator to check their pen and paper calculations or to help them identify their own mistakes. Calculators are also useful because they enable learners to access more realistic, and possibly more complex, everyday life problems. It is important to ensure learners have the skills to input correct key sequences and to interpret calculator displays correctly. Functional Skills maths tests require students to use a calculator and GCSE maths exams comprise both a calculator and a non-calculator paper. It is therefore important that learners are supported to use a calculator efficiently.

Terminology

In order to understand and use maths effectively, it is necessary to learn an extensive new vocabulary. Some terms are unique to maths while others are familiar words that are used in maths in a quite specific way. Unique maths words, such as parallelogram, need to be taught specifically and reinforced regularly. Everyday words that also have a mathematical meaning, such as odd, need to be identified and explained in a maths context. English words with multiple meanings can present particular difficulties for ESOL learners. Practising relevant key terminology in context is useful in helping to develop learners' understanding and confidence in using technical language.

Word problems

Even when learners have a good understanding of a mathematical concept, they can become confused when it is presented in the form of a worded question. Functional mathematics questions are set in context and may contain the names of people or places with which learners are not familiar. The context of the problem provides background information, but this can interfere with the information that is needed in order to solve the maths problem. Learners need to separate the essential information that is required to solve the problem from any surplus information that can be discarded. When we solve problems in real life, we do not have as much surplus information because we already understand the context. For example, standing in the paint aisle of a DIY store, we already know where we are and which room we want to paint. The only information we need to work out is whether we need one or two tins of paint. Some learners may prefer a pictorial representation to help set the context, whereas others will find this is a further distraction.

Learners need to understand the vocabulary in context, rather than just interpret individual words. For many learners, maths learning has been a solitary process. Although it is necessary for us to build our own understanding of concepts, processing mathematical ideas and concepts through dialogue with others can be helpful for some learners.

Embedding reminders

To help develop your learners' confidence in communicating mathematically:

✓ Encourage learners to practise using mathematical terms in place of informal everyday language when they are explaining concepts in whole group and small group discussion activities.

✓ Be aware of words that have a dual meaning in maths. If learners query maths terminology or meaning during your lesson, challenge them to find and explain other words that have a different meaning in maths.

✓ Providing lists of vocabulary will be unhelpful if the words are not linked to situations and reinforced with different activities, preferably in real-life contexts.

Each of the following maths chapters contains a brief focus on mathematical terminology and examples of some of the key vocabulary associated with each area.

Further reading

Basic Skills Agency (2001) *Adult Numeracy Core Curriculum*. London: DfES.

Casey, H., Cara, O., Eldred, J. et al. (2006) *You Wouldn't Expect a Maths Teacher to Teach Plastering*. London: NRDC.

Ofqual (2011) *Functional Skills Criteria for Mathematics*. Available at https://www.gov.uk/government/publications/functional-skills-criteria-for-mathematics.

8 Focusing on number

Reflective Task

Think about the different words you know that mean:

- Add
- Subtract
- Multiply
- Divide
- Do a question

You will find some suggestions at the end of the chapter.

Introduction

Addition, subtraction, multiplication and division are sometimes referred to as the four operations or the four basic operations. They are also referred to as the four rules of maths and are usually represented by the four symbols +, −, × and ÷. The reflective task above highlights that there is a range of vocabulary that can be used to represent each of the symbols. If learners are not familiar with the different terminology that is sometimes used in worded maths problems, they may misinterpret the question and select the wrong operation. One of the difficulties in solving worded maths problems is translating the words into mathematics.

Embedding idea

The activity above can be used as a small group activity with a class of learners, with each small group considering one of the operations. The activity should help to familiarize learners with some of the different words that can be used for each operation. Most problem-solving activities will involve learners in using one or more of these four operations.

Think about some of the other benefits this activity might have for learners who need to re-engage with mathematics.

- Talking about the words used for different operations is a non-threatening activity that provides opportunities for learners who are anxious about doing maths to just talk about it. They are only required to find words; there is no expectation for them to 'do' anything with numbers.
- The activity can also provide space for learners to express their thoughts and feelings about maths. It can be a useful starter activity at the beginning of a lesson or a module that will involve some calculations.

Mathematical terminology

Task 8.1

Consider the meaning of each of the words in Figure 8.1. Either write an explanation of the word in everyday life and then write the mathematical meaning, or use a drawing or diagram to help illustrate the different meanings.

	Meaning in everyday life	Mathematical meaning
Point		
Root		
Product		
Odd		
Table		

Figure 8.1 Mathematical words with different meanings in everyday life

> **Embedding idea**
>
> Challenge learners to find and explain other words that have a different meaning in mathematics.

General issues for ESOL learners

Apart from specialized maths terminology, there may be other issues that impede an ESOL learner's access to and comprehension of mathematics. ESOL learners may not be familiar with reading from left to right, they may use different methods for calculating and different symbols for numerals – for example, the Bengali symbol for 4 looks like the digit we use for the number 8. Many European and South American countries use a comma to indicate a decimal point. In the UK and North America, the decimal point is shown as a dot, and a comma or a space is commonly used to separate groups of thousands in large numbers. To add further confusion, some countries that use a comma to represent the decimal point, separate thousands with a dot.

Issues with maths terminology for ESOL learners

The spelling and pronunciation of number words can appear inconsistent, for example three and thirty, four and forty. Some number words can also be confused with everyday words that sound the same: counting from one to ten will highlight four number words that have different meanings in everyday life. Some ESOL learners may struggle with the meaning of the words in both contexts, and will have different words for each concept.

Many of the strategies that are useful for supporting ESOL learners to develop their maths vocabulary are also helpful for first language English speakers who are not familiar with maths terminology.

> **Embedding ideas**
>
> ✓ Provide plenty of opportunities for learners to use maths vocabulary.
> ✓ Make use of real-life examples.
> ✓ Integrate learners' cultural knowledge into learning.
> ✓ Connect to and build on prior knowledge.
> ✓ Integrate new words and paraphrase to encourage learners to develop their use of maths vocabulary.

Encourage learners to:

✔ Identify unknown words.
✔ Cross through the words associated with the contextual information that interferes with the maths.
✔ Sketch maths pictures and diagrams that help to illustrate the question.

Worded problems

A bricklayer has calculated that he needs 480 blocks to complete a one-storey extension. His boss has told him that he has to allow for 5% wastage. How many blocks should he order?

As part of their focused study, a group of 117 fine art students will be visiting the National Portrait Gallery. They will be accompanied by 8 lecturers, and will all be travelling by coach. Each coach can seat 46 passengers. How many coaches will they need for the trip?

Worded problems are most likely to contain information about the context as well as the mathematics. Learners will need to read through the question carefully and usually at least three times, to help ensure the correct information has been extracted and then used in an appropriate way. It is helpful to first skim through the question to help establish the context. Then slower reading is usually needed so that the information can be processed. A final read-through should check that the solution is sensible and answers the original question.

These stages can be viewed as three interrelated processes. First, learners need to be able to understand the situation by working out what to do; they need to decide what is relevant and plan what maths to use. The second step involves them in doing some maths in order to obtain a solution, but they still need to check back to confirm that their calculations are relevant and fulfil the requirement of the first step. The third step requires learners to interpret their solution in the context of the problem and to decide whether the answer is reasonable. If it is not, they should start again, and this can be demotivating for the non-mathematician.

To help set the context, it is a good idea to introduce and briefly explain the task to the learners. This helps them to process the first step in understanding the situation. For example, 'Today we are going to look at booking appointments for clients in the hair salon'. Another way to support this is to ask the learners what skills they think they will need and to try to draw out relevant vocabulary.

Small group collaborative activities will provide learners with the opportunity to discuss their different methods and to become aware that perhaps there are other, more efficient methods that they may wish to try in order to extend their own skills base. Encourage learners to discuss and share the strategies that they use with their peers.

To help support learners to structure their work and develop a systematic approach to problem-solving, it can be helpful to provide a problem-solving template (see Figure 8.2). These can be laminated so that learners can record and update their workings in the 'Do' column with a whiteboard marker. Templates can easily be wiped clean and re-used. Alternatively, learners could use a paper copy for each problem.

Step	Think about	Try out	Do
Identify the problem	What am I being asked to do? What information is given? Do I need more information? Is there anything I don't understand?	Write the problem in my own words Explain the problem to someone else	
Plan	Can I simplify the problem? Will a diagram help? Which calculations do I need to use? Have I solved a similar problem in the past?	Record your ideas Draw a picture or sketch a diagram	
Work through the problem	Translate your plan	Use a systematic approach Estimate an answer Carry out the calculations $+, -, \times, \div$ Check the calculations Check the plan	
Interpret the answer	Does the answer make sense? Is it close to my estimate? Have I answered the question?	If the answer is sensible, check with someone else If the answer is not sensible, look back at the question and your plan	

Figure 8.2 Problem-solving template

Mistakes and misconceptions

Learners make mistakes in maths for a variety of reasons, including careless-ness or a lack of concentration, working in haste and not reading the question properly or perhaps applying the wrong procedure. When an incorrect answer is identified, learners are often able to find their own mistakes and self-correct their work. Encouraging learners to check their work to identify mistakes is useful in helping them to recall and avoid a similar mistake in the future. It can also help highlight to the learner where marks may be lost in an assessment and that they need to check that they have fully answered the question. In some situ-ations, it is difficult for learners to spot their mistakes. For example, some learn-ers have difficulty reading and copying numbers and may transpose them. This means they reverse the order of the digits, so may write the number 365 as 356.

Misconceptions are much more interesting and give a feel for what learn-ers are thinking. A misconception arises from a concept that has worked on previous occasions, but is now misapplied. For example, a learner may 'see' that when multiplying by 10, whole numbers have a zero added to the right-hand side. In their experience, this rule has always worked. When applied to deci-mals, however, this rule can lead learners to think that $4.6 \times 10 = 4.60$. Learners without a secure sense of place value may not recognize that 4.6 and 4.60 are different representations of the same amount.

There are many typical misconceptions that teachers of mathematics are aware of and know to look out for. This is not a finite set and learners will con-tinue to apply their own rules and create new misconceptions. Part of the fun of maths teaching is exposing, unpicking and addressing learner misconceptions. Vocational teachers are not expected to have the same level of awareness of or enthusiasm about the misconceptions that their learners make, but there are some key typical learner responses that it will be helpful for you to be aware of when you are reinforcing maths concepts or checking your learners' work.

The examples in Figure 8.3 illustrate one typical error for each operation. It is important to recognize that the explanation suggested for each example is just one possibility. The most effective way to find out how your learners have approached a calculation is to talk to them and ask them to show you the steps they used.

It is important to develop a supportive learning environment that encour-ages learners to view mathematical mistakes and misconceptions as impor-tant learning opportunities, rather than something they have done wrong.

Mathematical misconceptions can be usefully exposed through learner dis-cussions during small group activities. You can gain useful insight into learner thinking by encouraging the learners to explore mathematical scenarios or situations and endeavouring to explain their thinking. A set of statement cards (Figure 8.4) can be used for this type of small group activity, with learners hav-ing to agree if and when a statement is true and to provide a justification for their decision. The activity usually works well with groups of three learners.

Operation	Error	Possible explanation	Strategy
Addition	$2.6 + 3.5 = 5.11$	The units and tenths have been added separately, leading to confusion in representing 11/10	Link to money and show £2.60 + £3.50. Use a decimal number line or a ruler marked in cm and mm to practise counting-on
Subtraction	$\begin{array}{r} 35 \\ -\,17 \\ \hline 22 \end{array}$	The smaller number has been subtracted from the larger number in each column. This may stem from learners attempting to find the difference. The strategy works for the whole number, but is more complex if each column is considered separately	Encourage the learner to identify the error by reinforcing that subtraction is the opposite of addition. Check using addition: 22 + 17 will not equal 35. Reinforce that 35 – 17 is not the same as 37 – 15
Multiplication	$\begin{array}{r} 21 \\ \times\,13 \\ \hline 63 \\ 21 \\ \hline 84 \end{array}$	Again, this is fundamentally a place value issue. The learner needs to recognize that they are multiplying by 13, not by 3 and 1 (or vice versa)	If a learner finds it difficult to remember the sequence of steps in this traditional approach, it may be helpful to encourage them to use an alternative method, such as the lattice method
Division	$10 \div \tfrac{1}{2} = 5$	Division can be seen as sharing equally. 20 divided by 5 can be represented as sharing 20 apples between 5 people. Sharing by ½ is not as intuitive	Refer to the reflective task at the beginning of this chapter and consider a different way of thinking about division. Perhaps think about how many fives go into 20 and then transfer to the number of halves in 10
Place value	0.25 is greater than 0.6	A greater number of digits implies a greater value. This works for whole numbers: 25 is greater than 6, therefore 0.25 must be greater than 0.6	Money is a useful representation for decimals with two decimal places. Consider the analogy of placing words in alphabetical order – look for the largest digit from left to right after the decimal point

Figure 8.3 Examples of learner errors

When you double a number, you always get an even number	The more digits a number has, the larger its value	$a \div b = a\overline{)b}$
2 + 3 = 5 + 5 = 10	Square numbers are always even numbers	When you multiply by 10, you add a zero to the right-hand side of the number

Figure 8.4 Number statement cards for discussion

Whole numbers

Strategies for calculating using the four basic operations

There are many different methods that can be used for adding, subtracting, multiplying and dividing numbers, so it is highly likely that your learners will use a variety of different approaches. Some people will find a method that works for them and stick to it; others will select different strategies depending on the size of the numbers. It is usual for different strategies to be used for mental calculations than for calculations carried out on paper. Deciding which strategy to use will also depend on the subject knowledge and confidence of each learner. Competence in manipulating numbers and efficient problem-solving skills rely on the ability to select effective and efficient methods of calculation:

- An **effective** method should produce a correct answer.
- An **efficient** method should generate a correct answer with minimum effort.

The key here is having a range of different methods to draw on, so you can select the most efficient for the task in hand.

Some learners will carry out calculations competently in their heads. Although this should be encouraged, they also need to be able to record the different steps in mental calculations in written maths assessments. Functional Skills maths requires learners to show or explain the methods they have used to calculate real-life problems. GCSE maths papers also contain functional questions that require learners to explain how and why they have selected a certain calculation. It is therefore useful to encourage learners to think about *how* they have calculated, rather than just praising a correct answer.

Before starting a topic that will involve learners in using calculations, it can be useful to check the different strategies that they employ. Sharing different calculation methods is a useful way for the teacher and the learners to check efficient pen-and-paper methods and provides time for learners to practise and hone a method that they may not have used for some time. It is also useful for encouraging learners to practise skills and develop confidence in using mental calculation strategies. Learners who are not confident with their current methods have an opportunity to learn alternative strategies from peers.

Before considering how your learners calculate, it is useful to think about the strategies you use, and whether you may be able to develop some alternative approaches so that you are in the best position to support your learners.

Some people will default to pen-and-paper methods because they feel more secure working methodically through a procedure. This is fine, but think about developing your – and ultimately your learners' – repertoire of available

---

Task 8.2

Think about how you approach the following calculations. Then refer to the Functional Skills coverage grid in Table 7.1 (p. 80) to decide which of the following are appropriate for students working at Entry Level 3:

1. $138 + 53$
2. $307 - 198$
3. 150×46
4. $240 \div 15$

---

methods to help enhance their problem-solving skills. Pen-and-paper methods carried out accurately are usually effective, but they may not be the most efficient approach.

Listed below are examples of some different approaches to the calculations. The examples are not exhaustive and it is likely that you have used a different and equally valid method.

Addition: 138 + 53

The example shown in part (a) uses a traditional approach that arranges the digits in columns, adding the units first, followed by the tens, then the hundreds:

$$\text{a)} \quad \begin{array}{r} 138 \\ +53 \\ \hline \\ \end{array} \quad \begin{array}{r} 138 \\ +53 \\ \hline 1 \\ {\scriptstyle 1} \end{array} \quad \begin{array}{r} 138 \\ +53 \\ \hline 91 \\ {\scriptstyle 1} \end{array} \quad \begin{array}{r} 138 \\ +53 \\ \hline 191 \\ {\scriptstyle 1} \end{array}$$

Examples (b) and (c) illustrate strategies that may be used for mental addition. When calculating mentally, we often partition and combine numbers in a different way, depending on the properties of each number. For example, in part (b) we could *hold* 138 in our heads, then add on 5 tens, then the 3 units. Part (c) shows that we may prefer to add the units before the tens. The order of adding tens or units makes no difference to the result and is mostly dependent on learner preference.

b) $138 + 50 + 3$ $138 + 50 = 188$

                              $188 + \ \ 3 = 191$

c) $138 + \ \ 3 + 50$ $138 + \ \ 3 = 141$

                              $141 + 50 = 191$

Part (d) uses rounding to the nearest 10 and then adjustment to compensate for the differences. Note that if we were asked to estimate the answer, we would stop after the initial rounding and wouldn't need to compensate.

d) $140 + 50 - 2 + 3$ $140 + 50 = 190$

                              $190 - \ \ 2 = 188$

                              $188 + \ \ 3 = 191$

Part (e) uses an empty number line to sketch and record the jumps that you may be able to do in your head. Learners who are not confident in calculating mentally may prefer a method that enables them to record each step.

e)

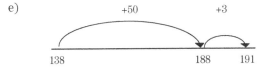

Subtraction: 307 – 198

Part (a) shows a typical column approach to subtraction that uses decomposition. This works by decomposing (or breaking up) the 300 so that we can work with 200 and 90 and 10. This is illustrated by use of the superscript numbers in the appropriate columns.

a) $\begin{array}{r} 3\ 0\ 7 \\ -1\ 9\ 8 \\ \hline \end{array}$ $\begin{array}{r} {}^{2\ 9}3\ \theta\ {}^{1}7 \\ -1\ 9\ 8 \\ \hline \ \ 9 \end{array}$ $\begin{array}{r} {}^{2\ 9}3\ \theta\ {}^{1}7 \\ -1\ 9\ 8 \\ \hline 0\ 9 \end{array}$ $\begin{array}{r} {}^{2\ 9}3\ \theta\ {}^{1}7 \\ -1\ 9\ 8 \\ \hline 1\ 0\ 9 \end{array}$

You may have spotted that, as 198 is almost 200, you can take away 200 and then add on 2 units to compensate.

b) $307 - 198$ $307 - 200 = 107$

$107 + 2 = 109$

Alternatively, you might have started with the lower number and counted up to the larger number, as shown in (c).

c) $198 \rightarrow 307$ $198 + \mathbf{2} = 200$

$200 + \mathbf{107} = 307$ $2 + 107 = 109$

The calculation in part (c) can also be represented by using a blank number line to count up in chunks from 198 to 307. This approach finds the difference between 198 and 307 by using addition, rather than subtraction.

d)

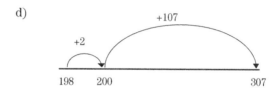

Alternatively, the blank number line can be used to count backwards from 307 as shown in (e).

e)

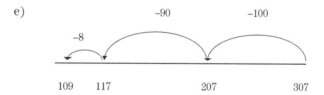

Multiplication: 150 × 46

Once again, part (a) shows one approach for a standard long multiplication calculation.

a)

	1 5 0	1 5 0	1 5 0	1 5 0
	× 4 6	× 4 6	× 4 6	× 4 6
	9 0 0	9 0 0	9 0 0	9 0 0
	—	—	6 0 0 0	6 0 0 0
	—	—	—	6 9 0 0

Parts (b) and (c) illustrate how the same calculation might be worked out mentally. Each step could also be illustrated with the use of informal jottings to help record each stage.

a) $150 \times 40 + 150 \times 6$

$150 \times 40 = 6000$

$150 \times \underline{6} = \underline{900}$

$150 \times \underline{46} = \underline{6900}$

b) $100 \times 46 + 50 \times 46$

$100 \times 46 = 4600$

$\underline{50} \times 46 = \underline{2300}$

$\underline{150} \times 46 = \underline{6900}$

Part (d) shows the lattice method of multiplication that is based on Napier's bones. The lattice method is sometimes referred to as a new method for multiplication, but the idea has been around since at least the middle of the last millennium. Napier's bones consist of a set of rods, with each rod representing a column of the multiplication tables. The rods can be combined in such a way as to enable multiplication calculations to be carried out by adding along the diagonals. The lattice method organizes the digits so they can be combined in a similar way; however, the learner will need to recall the multiplication tables in order to enter the digits.

d)

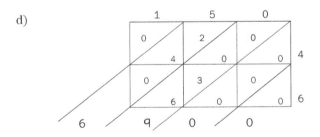

Part (d) is an example of a 3-digit number multiplied by a 2-digit number, so comprises 6 rectangles, one for each calculation. Each rectangle separates the solution for a single multiplication in two parts by a diagonal line. The 10s value is placed above the diagonal line and the units part below. For example, $5 \times 4 = 20$. The 2 is placed above the diagonal line and the 0 below. Track down the digits shaded in the middle diagonal to see how the digits are added to provide the solution.

This method is taught in schools, so you will most likely find that it is familiar to some of your learners. It looks quite complicated to set up, but then each step only requires the multiplication of one-digit numbers. It is a very efficient and useful method for learners who cannot remember the sequence for standard long multiplication. If you haven't seen the method used before, it would be advisable to begin with a 2-digit number multiplied by a 1-digit number, progressing to a 2-digit multiplied by a 2-digit number, before attempting the 3-digit by 2-digit example shown here, in order to build up an understanding of the way the digits are added down the diagonals to produce the answer.

Division: 240 ÷ 15

Part (a) shows a standard method for division, sometimes called the bus stop method.

a) $15 \overline{)2\,4^9 0}^{\,1}$ $15 \overline{)2\,4^9 0}^{\,1\,6}$

Parts (b) and (c) illustrate different ways of mentally working out how many 15s go into 240, using known facts.

b) $15 \times 10 = 150$

    $15 \times 5 = 75$

    $15 \times 1 = \underline{15}$

         $\underline{240}$ $10 + 5 + 1 = 16$

c) $15 \times 4 = 60$

    $60 \times 4 = 240$ $4 \times 4 = 16$

One of the issues that may arise if learners confine themselves to using a standard written method for calculations, as illustrated in part (a) of each of the examples, is that this does not encourage them to develop a sense of the size of the numbers they are calculating. For example, considering the addition calculation 138 + 53, learners can mechanically add 8 and 3 (units), then add 3 and 5 (tens), and then carry down the 1 (hundred). They don't need to think about the size of either number, or develop their skills in estimating. Carelessly misaligned numbers are very likely to result in the wrong answer.

Similarly with the standard long multiplication procedure, it is quite common for learners to forget to place a zero in the units column when multiplying by the 10s digit. Without an understanding of the size of the numbers, it is difficult for learners to recognize that an answer may not be reasonable. To help overcome this, learners should be encouraged to estimate: adding *about 140* to *about 50* should give an answer that is *about 190*. Some of the mental calculation strategies illustrated may help learners develop an appreciation of the size of the numbers and therefore be more likely to recognize when an answer is reasonable.

Number facts

Efficient methods do not simply rely on knowing a procedure for addition, subtraction, multiplication and division, but also depend on an understanding of the different relationships that numbers have with each other. Recall of common number bonds, the multiplication tables and a clear sense of place value are all tools that help build up the bank of useful facts that contribute to the development of efficient calculation strategies. For example, if we know $6 \times 8 = 48$, we can derive $12 \times 8 = 96$ and $24 \times 8 = 192$. If calculating $9 + 26$, it makes sense to start with the larger number and count on the smaller number. We also need to learn that the order for subtraction and division cannot be reversed in the same way that it can for addition and multiplication.

Number bonds

Number bonds to 10 are the pairs of numbers that are added together to make 10. For example: 1 and 9, 2 and 8, 3 and 7.

You might have made use of number bonds to 10 when calculating the addition question above: $138 + 53$. If you know that 8 and 2 make 10, then 8 and 3 must make one more than 10. Thus there is one 10 to carry forward, and 1 left to record in the units column.

Bonds to 10 can be usefully extended to bonds to 20. This necessitates attaching the word 'teen' to one half of the bond, but also adds a complication with the inconsistency for eleven and twelve.

Bonds to 100 are a further extension, using 10 and 90, 20 and 80 and then developing to include digits that are not multiples of 10, such as 75 and 25, 82 and 18.

Place value

Place value refers to the value of the place (or position) of a digit within a number. In the decimal system, we use ten different digits and rely on the position of each digit to tell us the number. An understanding of the place value system is essential for being able to work out the size of a number and for developing skills in estimating.

Learners should be presented with a realistic context for reading very large and very small numbers. For example, scientists can compare the size of atoms and cells or the distance between planets. Learners on an information technology course can consider the sizes of computer hard drives in gigabytes and terabytes and the speed of processing in nanoseconds.

Rounding numbers to the nearest ten or hundred provides a good introduction to estimating. Skills in estimation are useful for mental calculations and for being able to recognize whether an answer is sensible. Learners are often reluctant to estimate because they think they need to produce a correct answer. Some will provide an exact solution to quite complex calculations when asked to estimate an answer. If they don't recognize the importance of being able to estimate an answer, they are unlikely to develop the skills required to help them make quick mental calculations in everyday budgeting activities. Newspapers are a useful source for finding headline figures that have been rounded in a particular way.

Temperature change can provide a practical context for working with negative numbers. Learners involved in catering or health and social care can consider safe fridge and freezer temperatures. It is beneficial if learners are able to use real equipment for reading temperature scales on a range of different equipment. The scale on a thermometer provides a useful number line for reading across zero.

Looking at bank balances and bank statements provides another everyday application of negative numbers that can be relevant to learners across most vocational contexts. Interpreting a bank balance also introduces a range of new terminology, for example being in the red or black and in credit or debit.

Decimals, fractions and percentages

This is one of the areas where many learners struggle. Competence in using fractions, decimals and percentages relies on a secure understanding of the four rules. In particular, it is difficult to work comfortably with fractions without some proficiency in recognizing number patterns and recalling multiplication and division facts.

It is common for learners to view fractions, decimals and percentages as unrelated topics. They tend to view them as discrete topics and attempt to apply particular rules to each of them. In some situations, it can be useful to move between the different representations, and a card matching activity can help to illustrate that they are just different ways of showing the same thing.

A card matching or sorting activity can be a useful introduction to a lesson that contains work on fractions, decimals or percentages. Learners should work in small groups and be encouraged to justify their matching. This should promote discussion between them and enable you to begin to identify any gaps in understanding or learner misconceptions.

A set of equivalence cards that includes the fraction representation in words is useful for all learners, but particularly for ESOL learners (Figure 8.5). Some learners may say 'three-fourths' rather than three-quarters as they extend their understanding that 1/10 is pronounced as one-tenth. Using the word *fourths* instead of *quarters* will not affect a learner's conceptual

$\frac{1}{3}$	$0.\dot{3}$	$33\frac{1}{3}\%$	one-third
$\frac{3}{10}$	0.3	30%	three-tenths
$\frac{1}{2}$	0.5	50%	one-half
$\frac{3}{4}$	0.75	75%	three-quarters
$\frac{2}{5}$	0.4	40%	two-fifths

Figure 8.5 Set of cards to match equivalent fractions, decimals and percentages

understanding or their ability to calculate, but may inhibit their general understanding if they are not familiar with the written word or the spoken term.

It is useful for learners to know some of the common equivalences between fractions, decimals and percentages, so they can consider alternative approaches to calculations. They are unlikely, however, to value tasks that require conversions between fractions, decimals and percentages for no reason other than to provide practice. In a practical situation, reasoning about why a particular format has been selected would be more useful and could lead to a purposeful group discussion that compares different representations.

Class attributes can be a useful way for learners to see a practical application of fractions. You might refer to the fraction of the group who travel to college by bus, or the fraction of students who eat a main meal in the college canteen. Some fractions can be translated easily into percentages and, depending on the level of your group, this may be part of the challenge. The key thing here is for learners to appreciate which representation is used realistically in an everyday situation. For example:

If an apple pie is cut into five equal pieces, we could say we have one-fifth of the pie. We are unlikely to say we have 20% or 0.2 of the pie, as this would be an unnatural way to use equivalence.

If nine out of fifteen learners travel by bus, we could also represent this as a percentage: $9/15 = 3/5 = 60/100 = 60\%$. The percentage and the fraction are both sensible representations, since we can say that 60% or 3/5 of the group travel by bus. In this situation, the decimal representation is not realistic, as we would not say that 0.6 of the group travel by bus.

Task 8.3

Consider practical representations in different contexts:

a) Is a stage production team more likely to refer to an area on stage in terms of a fraction, a decimal or a percentage amount of the whole stage?

b) How might a sports centre manager represent an increase or decrease in membership rates?

We tend to use fractions and percentages when making a comparison. Decimals are generally used for money and measurement.

It is helpful to make links across topics and real-life situations to encourage learners to develop their conceptual understanding of a quantity. For example, consider the different representations for a half:

½, 0.5, 50%, also ½ a kilo is 500 g, ½ an hour is 30 minutes, ½ a pound might mean 8 oz or 50 p, depending on the context.

Money is often used to introduce decimals. It is important to check that learners know the decimal point separates the pounds from pence, or the whole numbers from the decimal part. It is helpful to refer to other decimal representations when reading decimal numbers. Reading the decimal 3.75, we would read *three point seven five*. With money, we say £3.75 as *three pounds seventy-five*. Measuring a wall in metres, we read 3.75 m as *three point seven five metres* or as *3 metres and 75 cm*.

Figure 8.6 provides another discussion activity using statements that students can discuss in small groups and agree as either true or false, providing a clear justification for their decision. This approach encourages students to use reasoning and explain their thinking, and again provides the teacher with an opportunity to identify and address typical student misconceptions.

$\frac{2}{5}$ is smaller than $\frac{1}{3}$	$\frac{1}{5}$ is the same as 0.2
$0.75 + 0.25 = 0.100$	$\frac{1}{3} + \frac{1}{3} = \frac{2}{6}$
$\frac{3}{10}$ is the same as 30%	$\frac{1}{4}$ is the same as $\frac{4}{12}$

Figure 8.6 Fraction, decimal and percentage statement discussion cards

Reflective task – suggestions

Suggestions for some of the different words that can be used for add, subtract, multiply, do a question are shown in Figure 8.7.

+	–	×	÷	*Do*
Addition	Subtraction	Multiplication	Division	Solve
Plus	Minus	Times	Split	Find
Increase	Decrease	Lots of	Goes into	Evaluate
Sum	Difference	Product	Share equally	Calculate
More than	Take away	By	Divided by	Estimate
Total	Remove	Repeated addition	Divided into	Convert

Figure 8.7

Worded problems – solutions

a) 480 blocks + 5%

 10% of 480 = 48

 5% of 480 = 24

 Builder needs to order 480 + 24 = 504 blocks.

b) 117 + 8 = 125 passengers

 125 ÷ 46 = 2.717...

 Round up, so 3 coaches are needed.

Further reading

Department for Education and Skills (DfES) (2007) *Thinking Through Mathematics: Strategies for Teaching and Learning.* London: NRDC.
Swan, M. (2005) *Improving Learning in Mathematics: Challenges and Strategies.* Sheffield: DfES Standards Unit.

A series of short books promoting practical approaches to teaching mathematics from Maths4Life are available at http://www.nrdc.org.uk/?cat=7:

Bouch, D. and Ness, C. (2007) *Maths4Life: Measurement.* London: NRDC.
McLeod, R. and Newmarch, B. (2006) *Maths4Life: Fractions.* London: NRDC.
Ness, C. and Bouch, D. (2007) *Maths4Life: Time and Money.* London: NRDC.
Ness, C. and Bouch, D. (2007) *Maths4Life: Topic Based Teaching.* London: NRDC.
Newmarch, B. and Part, T. (2007) *Maths4Life: Number.* London: NRDC.

9 Measure, shape and space

Reflective Task

Two students are discussing their training routines. They have both been running and are now comparing their average speeds.

A: I was going at my usual speed. I always pace myself to run steady 10-minute miles.

B: I ran for 30 minutes this morning and covered exactly 5 kilometres.

A: So I'm still running faster than you then!

Is A right?

Use the fact that 5 miles is approximately equal to 8 kilometres. You will find the answer at the end of the chapter.

Introduction

This chapter addresses when we measure things at work and in everyday life. Measurement involves a number and a unit. For example, to say that a jug holds 2 is meaningless until we link a unit to the number. The jug holds 2 litres, 2 cups or 2 pints provides more information, but for the information to be meaningful we need to develop an understanding, or a sense of the size of a measure. One aspect of measuring sense involves being able to select an appropriately sized unit to match what we are measuring; another is being able to gauge a rough estimate for what we are measuring. The reflective task provides an example of how you need to do both of these things.

Your learners will need to be able to use measurement for a variety of different tasks in their vocational settings. It is important to support the development of their mathematical knowledge in this area so that they can fulfil their role competently. In this chapter, we will look at a number of different vocational subject areas and how measurement might feature in the tasks needed to work in this area.

The chapter is structured so that you can see real examples of the use of measurement before identifying the mathematical principles underpinning that use. Each section provides a contextualized example of using measurement and the idea is that through considering the examples, you will come to realize which mathematical concepts are needed. As you work through the examples, try not to worry about whether the maths is obvious to you. In the second half of the chapter, some of the basic concepts needed are presented with further examples and tasks. The best way to read the chapter is to consider each vocationally situated area first and then check the concepts in the second part of the chapter.

Measure

Consider the following examples and think about how you can adapt some of the ideas for use in your own specialist area.

Measurement in health and social care

In the adult health and social care sector, care workers provide care and support for people in residential and nursing homes, day centres or clients' own homes.

In a typical day at work, a care worker's responsibilities may include:

- Efficient time management: use the 12- and 24-hour clock; add and subtract units of time; estimate time and round time to the nearest 10 or 15 minutes.
- Completing weight and fluid charts: recognize and use metric and imperial systems; convert between metric and imperial measures; weigh, record and calculate weight loss or gain.
- Planning nutritional requirements: calculate calorie intakes; interpret nutritional values tables and guideline daily amounts on food packets.
- Kitchen health and safety: know safe fridge and freezer temperatures.
- Managing money.

Ideas for reinforcing time

Begin by finding out what the learners already know. Ask them the different ways they know to record the time (e.g. 1.45 pm, 13:45, ¼ to 2 in the afternoon) to check how familiar they are with the 12- and 24-hour clock. Reading and recording time using the 12- and 24-hour clock is a Level 1 skill, so it is likely that entry-level learners may not be confident converting between the two formats.

If learners need practice in using the 12- and 24-hour clock, it can be helpful to use a set of time cards showing typical daily activities with the time written in different formats. Ask learners to work in pairs or small groups and to place the cards in time order. The activity time cards can be placed around an imaginary clock face to help reinforce the position of numbers on an analogue clock; alternatively, they can be placed in chronological order on the desk or stuck on a wall or whiteboard.

It is useful to include some additional blank cards for learners to complete and slot into their day's activities (see Figure 9.1). To extend the challenge, ask learners to work out length of time between each activity card.

Ten fifty-five pm	16:10	09:00	11.45 am
13:45		18:00	14:55
10.10 am	4.35 pm	12.30 pm	21:30
5.30 in the afternoon	08:30		9.15 am

Figure 9.1 12- and 24-hour clock cards

Time also includes knowing facts about dates and the calendar. Learners need to be familiar with the sequence of the months of the year to be able to read, record and understand dates in different formats. For example, 9th January 2016 can be recorded as: 09.01.16, 9/01/16, 9th Jan '16.

Ideas for weight or liquid measures

Start with what the learners know. You could ask them to identify the sorts of things that they measure in their daily lives, or to identify the different units that can be used to measure and record weight or liquids. Some adult learners might only use the imperial measurement system and will need to familiarize themselves with the metric system. Encourage them to sort between metric and imperial measures and then to discuss where each is commonly used.

Learners are often uncertain about the different sizes of metric measures and the relationship between the different units in the same system. Converting between grams and kilograms will rely on an understanding of the place value system and the ability to multiply and divide by 1000; similarly for converting between millilitres and litres. It may be necessary to look at the whole place value system to reinforce that the metric measuring system is based on powers of ten.

It is useful for learners to know rough conversions between some of the more commonly used imperial measures and the metric system, as this can help them to estimate sensible answers. More precise calculations will involve multiplying and dividing by decimals and so may require the use of a calculator, depending on the level of the learner.

The abbreviation for litre is l. In some printed fonts, this will appear as l and so can be confused with the number 1. Select fonts carefully and encourage learners to write l with a tail to represent litres.

Embedding ideas

✓ Provide real equipment for measuring – measuring jugs, bathroom and kitchen scales showing different numbered divisions are helpful for providing practice in reading and interpreting the divisions on different scales.
✓ Learners can misread scales because they assume that each division on the scale represents one unit.
✓ Develop a sense of the size of common measures by linking to familiar portion sizes and daily allowances. For example, how much liquid does a standard mug or cup hold? How many millilitres or centilitres in a bottle of water or a can of drink? What is the recommended daily intake for liquids – and approximately how many drinks are needed to maintain a healthy intake of fluid?
✓ Encourage learners to estimate before measuring.
✓ Encourage learners to become familiar with typical body weights for small, medium and large framed people or food portion sizes to help them develop confidence in thinking in metric. Figure 9.2 contains a sample weight chart.

Weight chart			
Name:			
Date	Weight (kg)	Loss (kg)	Gain (kg)
11 February	60.5		
18 February	59.7	0.8	
25 February	59.9		0.2
4 March			

Figure 9.2 Weight chart

Weight or mass?

When we want to measure how heavy something is, we tend to refer to this as the weight of an object. What we are in fact referring to is the mass of that object.

- **Mass** refers to how much matter is in an object and is generally measured in grams and kilograms, or pounds and ounces.
- **Weight** refers to the force (or gravitational pull) acting on an object and is measured in Newtons.

In everyday language, we tend to say *find the weight*, rather than *find the mass*. Some learners are likely to become confused if you refer to weighing activities as finding the mass. However, in some vocational areas it is important that learners understand the difference. Learners on maths, science and engineering courses, and of course trainee astronauts, will need to know the difference and will be expected to apply the correct technical terminology.

In real-life situations where we want learners to be functional in using their maths, we can adopt the language used in the Functional Skills Standards and the Adult Numeracy Core Curriculum. Both these documents refer to learners being able to estimate, measure, use and compare *weight*.

Throughout this chapter, I have used the term weight when referring to how heavy something is, in order to maintain this consistency.

Task 9.1

If you are working in a health and social care or related industry, consider how maths might be used in the following workplace scenarios:

a) Planning nutritional requirements.
b) Kitchen health and safety.
c) Managing money.

Measurement in the construction industry

Learners training to work in the construction industry will need to be able to:

- Measure and cut wallpaper, skirting board, pipes and cables.
- Calculate areas for painting, tiling or to lay laminate flooring.
- Measure and mix materials in ratio – for cement, plaster and paint.
- Produce and interpret floor plans, elevations and scale diagrams.

Ideas for length

Some of the ideas suggested above for weight and liquid measures will apply to length. Again, you will need to begin by finding out what your learners already know and whether they are familiar with the metric or imperial system, or both.

It is useful to connect standard measures with everyday objects. For example, an ordinary door in a house is approximately 2 metres high. From this a learner can deduce that a man cannot be 3.5 m tall, and can make rough estimates for the height and length of a room. Similarly, knowing that a fingernail is approximately 1 cm wide can help learners to estimate the length of smaller items.

Learners' skills in reading large or small numbers can be made more meaningful when linked to a real application. For example, construction students can be encouraged to read and compare the heights of some of the world's tallest buildings or longest bridges.

The term perimeter can be introduced when learners measure walls to calculate lengths of picture rail or skirting board. This can be associated with finding the perimeter of simple shapes.

Embedding ideas

✓ Some rulers and measuring tapes display both metric and imperial scales; the different scales can be a useful discussion point at the start of the lesson.
✓ Check measurements are taken from the notch for zero, rather than the end of the ruler.
✓ When counting we start at the number one; this can lead some learners to think they need to measure from the notch for the number 1.
✓ Make links between standard lengths and familiar objects.
✓ Check learners know what the notches between the whole numbers on a ruler represent.

Area and volume

Measuring length can be extended to calculating area and volume:

- Area uses two dimensions and so is measured in squared units, for example m^2.
- Volume uses three dimensions and is measured in cubic units, for example m^3.

Learners may begin by counting squares to find the area of simple rectangles. They need to progress to multiplying dimensions together to make their calculations more efficient and for application in a practical context, such as calculating an area of wall to decorate.

Some calculations are easier to manage if conversions between units are made before multiplying. For example, to work out the area of a wall with dimensions 3,500 mm × 4,000 mm, it is simpler to convert mm to metres before calculating 3.5 m × 4 m = 14 m^2.

Compare this with 3,500 mm × 4,000 mm = 14,000,000 mm^2. Learners are now confronted with having to convert mm^2 to m^2 and a common misconception here is to divide by 1,000 rather than correctly dividing by 1,000^2 or 1,000,000.

Encourage learners to estimate quantities before measuring accurately and to use their estimate to check whether their final answer is reasonable.

Learners often confuse the terms area and perimeter, so it can be helpful to reinforce the concepts by linking to everyday terms such as perimeter fence, which goes around the outside of an enclosed area.

Learners should be encouraged to engage in practical and realistic tasks that enable them to develop their conceptual understanding. For example, learners on an animal care course can measure cages and small animal enclosures, calculating areas and volumes to compare against the suggested RSPCA standards.

Example

The minimum cage size for two guinea pigs is 120 cm × 60 cm × 45 cm.

Sketch the cage.
What is the volume of the cage?
How much floor space do the animals have?
What other cage sizes will give the same floor area?
Justify whether your designs produce a safe cage for two guinea pigs.

Using ratio and direct proportion

Ratio and proportion are used in a variety of situations in everyday life as well as more specifically in different vocational areas. In the reflective task, runner A runs steady 10-minute miles, so in 20 minutes he would run 2 miles and in 30 minutes he would run 3 miles. This is an example of using direct proportion.

Example 1

If I need 250 g of rice for four servings, how much rice will I need for 6 people?

There are different ways to work this out:

a) Method 1: ½ × 250 g = 125 g (2 portions)   250 g + 125 g = 375 g
b) Method 2: 250 g ÷ 4 = 62.5 g (one portion)   62.5 g × 6 = 375 g

In real life, some people will measure by scooping out one cup of rice for 4 portions, and then add another half a cup for the extra two portions. Either approach will keep the quantities in direct proportion.

Example 2

A photographer needs to mix developer solution with water in a ratio of 1:5. If he uses 200 ml of developer, how much water should he use?

The order in which the solution and water appear in the question relates to the order of the numbers in ratio. For every one part of solution, the photographer needs 5 parts of water.

200 ml of developer represents one part, so 5 lots of 200 ml of water is needed:
5 × 200 ml = 1,000 ml = 1 litre

Depending on their vocational areas, learners might need to use direct proportion to scale recipes, calculate building materials for construction projects, blend colours for hair dye or work out currency exchange. To help engage and motivate learners, it is a good idea to introduce ratio or proportion problems that relate to their vocational area of interest. However, it is also important for learners to be able to transfer their understanding to less familiar situations to help prepare them for exams, when questions are likely to be set in a variety of different contexts.

Task 9.2

Think about how some of the suggestions above can be adapted for use in your own vocational area.

a) Hairdressers will need to be able to use an appointment booking system.
b) Scientists will need to be able to calculate the surface area of cells.
c) Dancers can make use of two-dimensional shapes to inspire body movement.

Cross-curricula ideas

Many practical everyday tasks involve the use of number and measure and can be used to help learners develop their skills and confidence in using maths in a meaningful way. Learners are more likely to take ownership of an activity or event if they are involved in planning it. This involvement can lead to a deeper and more secure understanding of the mathematical concepts because they are being applied to something relevant to the learner. If tutors plan a trip and present the details to the learners, it is a missed chance to use the opportunity to develop learners' maths skills.

One approach to involving the learners might be to introduce different aspects of the planning as part of a series of lesson starter activities. This can be particularly helpful to learners if used as a recap of recent prior learning. Alternatively, planning may be condensed into a couple of lessons with the learners doing some independent research between lessons.

Planning a whole-group trip

A trip to a museum, art gallery, theatre or sporting event may form part of the curriculum or be an end-of-term treat. In either case, it is beneficial to encourage learners to play an active part in the planning and preparation for the trip. Problem-solving, collating and organizing paperwork, negotiating with others, and planning to a fixed budget and a deadline, all involve valuable skills that are transferrable to a variety of different job roles as well as enhancing personal skills in managing time and money.

Financial planning
Costing the trip is likely to include transport and entry costs. Researching the cost of public transport could involve a comparison between train and coach travel and should consider discounts for group travel or student discount cards. Many public museums and art galleries have free entry. Sporting events and theatre trips are likely to involve an additional cost, but again there may be discounts for groups or for students.

Timing
Learners will need to consider journey times in order to help maximize the time spent at a venue or to ensure the group arrive with time to spare before the start of a production or a match.

Communication activity

This activity can be used to highlight the importance of clear two-way communication and the value in being able to ask questions. It is also a good opportunity to reinforce mathematical shape terminology. Start by finding out which shape names your learners know and are able to describe. It may be necessary to display some basic shapes alongside the shape names for them to refer to during the activity, or they may have demonstrated that they know a sufficient number of basic shapes to work from memory. It is usually a good idea to start with flat, two-dimensional shapes, but some learners may want to challenge each other by including solid shapes.

Learners should work in pairs and sit back-to-back. Ask the pair to elect A to give instructions and B to draw. They each should have a turn at giving instructions.

The instructor (A) needs to describe the design using the mathematical words for shape and position. They should not describe the shape or look to see what the drawer (B) is drawing until they have finished describing the drawing.

The drawer (B) follows the instructions. They should not see the design in advance or ask for repeat instructions.

Learners can compare drawings and then swap roles (Figure 9.3).

It is useful to ask learners to sketch their own designs to use. Some learners will draw intricate shapes and designs and may need reminding to use the correct mathematical terminology to describe their designs (Figure 9.4).

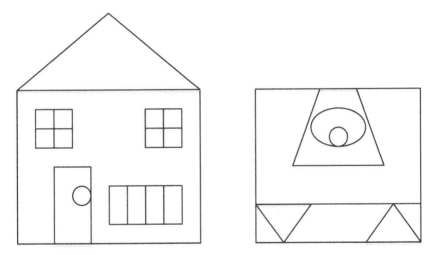

Figure 9.3 Communication activity using mathematical shapes

Shape name	Shape	Position
equilateral triangle		above
isosceles triangle		below
scalene triangle		to the right of
trapezium		to the left of
kite		in the centre
rhombus		horizontal
parallelogram		vertical
pentagon		at 90°
hexagon		parallel
octagon		perpendicular

Figure 9.4 Examples of shape and position terminology

Measure and shape terminology

Apart from the specialized symbols that are used in maths, we also use some technical words that have a precise mathematical meaning. Words such as *isosceles, quadrilateral* and *trapezium* are specific maths terms that need to be carefully explained and then reinforced regularly to ensure they become familiar.

Other technical terms have a different everyday meaning – words such as *face*, which can mean the front of the head but can also refer to the flat surface of a solid object, as in the face of a cube.

Sometimes different terminology is used for the same concept. Some learners have difficulty remembering the difference between area and perimeter, then, just as they grasp the idea that the perimeter represents the outside of a two-dimensional shape, they discover that the line around the outside of a circle is referred to as the circumference.

Dimensions for width and length can be ambiguous and may depend on the context. The sides of a square are generally referred to as lengths. The longer side of a rectangle is often referred to as the length and the shorter side as the width, as shown in Figure 9.5.

Figure 9.5

One of the practical applications of length and width is measuring windows to fit a pair of curtains. In this context, the term used for the measurement from top to bottom of the curtains varies between length, height and drop. Instructions for measuring across the window tend to refer to this dimension as the width.

Embedding reminders

✓ Introduce specific terminology in context and support with diagrams where possible.
✓ Reinforce technical terms regularly.

Issues for ESOL learners

ESOL learners may be unfamiliar with some of the everyday words and phrases used in English for approximation, such as 'more or less', 'just about' and 'roughly'. They may also be unfamiliar with the imperial measurement system that is still used in the UK and the contexts for using words such as pints, stones and pounds.

Basic concepts

This section contains some of the core concepts that your learners will need to understand. It is advisable to work through each of the challenges, as these are based on typical questions that often present difficulties for learners.

The metric system

The metric unit names without any prefixes are litre, metre and gram. Adding a prefix tells us how much of the unit is required. For example:

- milli is a prefix used to denote one-thousandth, so 1 millilitre is one-thousandth (1/1,000) of a litre;
- centi is a prefix used to denote one-hundredth, so 1 centimetre is one-hundredth (1/00) of a metre;
- kilo is a prefix used to denote one thousand, so 1 kilogram is one thousand (1,000) grams.

The prefix is consistent, so for example we always multiply by 1000 to convert kilogram to grams, or kilometres to metres. However, what can confuse learners is converting between two quantities that both have prefixes. For example, converting between millimetres and centimetres, or centimetres and kilometres. It is helpful to encourage learners to visualize and recall the size order within each system, and then to apply the conversion between each commonly used measure. For example, learners will need to know that the common metric measures for length are mm, cm, m, km – in that size order – and that there are 10 mm in 1 cm, 100 cm in 1 m, and 1,000 m in 1 km. Learners are then able to work from their knowledge of the metric system, rather than attempt to memorize all the possible conversions.

Example

A 10-pence piece has a diameter of 2.5 cm. Students collect 100,000 10-pence pieces for Children in Need. If they were to lay them end to end, how far would they reach?

Extension task: How much money have they raised for charity?

Distance covered is 2.5 cm × 100,000 = 250,000 cm.

Converting from 250,000 cm to kilometres (Figure 9.6).

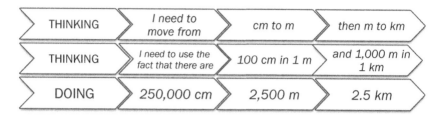

Figure 9.6 Working with the metric system

Area

- Area means the size of a surface or the space within a flat shape.
- Learners usually begin to work out the size of a square or rectangular surface by counting squares.
- Areas of shapes can also be found by multiplying two dimensions together, typically length × width.
- Area is always recorded in units squared, because it is 2-dimensional.

An area of one square centimetre measures 1 cm × 1 cm and is written as 1 cm². The area of the square in Figure 9.7 is 1 cm × 1 cm = 1 cm².

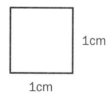

Figure 9.7

The formula for finding the area of a rectangle is length × width. The area of the rectangle in Figure 9.8 is 6 cm × 4 cm = 24 cm².

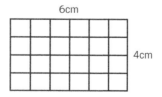

Figure 9.8

If you cut a rectangle in half along the diagonal, you get a triangle whose area is half that of the rectangle. The area of a triangle with base 6 cm and height 4 cm will be ½ the area of the 6 cm × 4 cm rectangle.

The formula for finding the area of a triangle is ½ × base × height . The area of the triangle in Figure 9.9 is ½ × 6 × 4 = 12 cm².

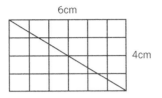

6cm

4cm

Figure 9.9

Area of composite shapes

More complex shapes can sometimes be divided into two or more basic shapes. These are called composite shapes (Figure 9.10).

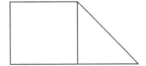

Figure 9.10

Challenge 1

An area of 1 square centimetre measures 1 cm by 1 cm. How many mm² are in 1 cm²? Select from:

a)   10
b)   100
c)   1,000

Volume

- Volume is the amount of space taken up by a solid object.
- The volume of a solid is calculated by multiplying three dimensions together.
- Volume is measured in cubic units, because it is 3-dimensional.

The 1 cm cube in Figure 9.11 has a volume of 1 cubic centimetre: 1 cm × 1 cm × 1 cm = 1 cm³.

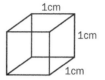

Figure 9.11

In much the same way that different terminology is used to represent the sides of a 2-dimensional shape, this inconsistency continues with 3-dimensional shapes. Terminology to represent the sides of a 3-dimensional shape could include length, depth and width, or length, breadth and height, or any combination of these terms.

The formula for finding the volume of a cuboid is length × width × height. The volume of the cuboid in Figure 9.12 is:

12 cm × 5 cm × 3 cm
= 60 × 3 cm³
= 180 cm³

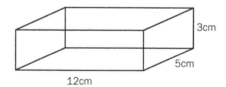

Figure 9.12

Challenge 2

One cubic metre measures 1 m × 1 m × 1 m. How many cubic centimetres are in one cubic metre? Select from:

a)   100   (one hundred)
b)   1,000   (one thousand)
c)   1,000,000   (one million)

Capacity

- Capacity is the amount of liquid a container can hold.
- Metric measures for capacity are the litre, centilitre and millilitre.
- Units of capacity are related to units of volume.

$$1 \text{ ml} = 1 \text{ cm}^3$$
$$1 \text{ litre} = 1{,}000 \text{ ml}$$
$$\text{so } 1 \text{ litre} = 1{,}000 \text{ cm}^3$$

Consider the 12 cm × 5 cm × 3 cm cuboid shown in Figure 9.12 as an open tank. Each 1 cm³ is equal to 1 ml, so the capacity of the open tank is 180 ml.

Challenge 3

What is the capacity of a tank with dimensions 1 m × 1 m × 1 m? Select from:

a)   1 litre   (1,000 ml)
b)   100 litres   (100,000 ml)
c)   1,000 litres   (1,000,000 ml)

Ratio

A ratio is a way to compare amounts.

A ratio of 2 parts to every 5 parts can be written as 2:5. We separate the parts with a colon and express it in words as the ratio of *two to five*.

Ratio can be scaled up. Multiply each part by the same factor.

2:5 is the same as 4:10 and 8:20 and 10:25

Ratio can be cancelled down, or simplified. Divide each part by the same factor.

20:50 is the same as 2:5

A day nursery needs 1 member of staff for every 3 children under the age of two.

The ratio of *staff* to *children* is written as 1:3
The ratio of *children* to *staff* is written as 3:1

A builder uses a 4:1 sand and cement mix for mortar.

The mortar mix uses 5 *parts* all together (4 sand + 1 cement)

The builder needs 25 kg of mortar. To calculate how much sand and cement he must use:

Find *1 part* by dividing total mix by number of parts: 25 kg ÷ 5 = 5 kg
4 parts of sand will need 4 × 5 kg = 20 kg sand
1 part cement will need 1 × 5 kg = 5 kg cement
Check totals: 20 kg + 5 kg = 25 kg

Challenge 4

The builder uses a 4:1 sand and cement mix for mortar. He has 3 bags of cement.
How many bags of sand will he need to make his mortar mix?

Reflective task – solution

A runs each mile in 10 minutes, so would run 5 miles in 50 minutes.
B runs each kilometre in 6 minutes, so would run 8 kilometres in 48 minutes.
So, as 5 miles is approximately equivalent to 8 kilometres, B is running faster than A.

Challenge 1 – solution

Answer: 100
10 × 10 = 100

Challenge 2 – solution

Answer: 1 million
100 × 100 × 100 = 1,000,000

Challenge 3 – solution

Answer: 1,000 litres
100 cm × 100 cm × 100 cm = 1,000,000 cm^3
1,000,000 cm^3 = 1,000,000 ml (1 cm^3 = 1 ml)
1,000,000 ml = 1000 litres (1000 ml = 1 litre)

Challenge 4 – solution

Answer: 12 bags sand (it doesn't matter what size the bags are, just that the same measure is used for each part).

10 Data handling

Reflective Task

Twenty people were asked three questions and their responses are recorded below. Think of a suitable question that could have been asked to produce each of the three following results:

Question 1: Yes, yes, yes, no, no, no, no, yes, no, yes, no, no, yes, yes, no, yes, no, no, no, yes.

Question 2: 53, 57, 65, 89, 62, 64, 54, 56, 58, 43, 75, 70, 68, 72, 57, 62, 66, 73, 58, 57.

Question 3: Red, blue, black, silver, green, green, blue, silver, white, white, blue, red, black, red, black, yellow, white, silver, red, blue.

The results presented here are an example of data in its raw form. The questions you have thought of will provide a context for each of the sets of data; some suggestions are provided at the end of the chapter. Now think about how you could present the data in a different way to make it appear more interesting and informative.

Introduction

This chapter looks at some of the different ways that data can be collected, represented and analysed. In everyday life, we are surrounded by information presented in a variety of different forms. Newspapers often display numerical information in charts and tables to support written text and to provide a visual impact. For example, an article that provides details about the ten highest-paid public service executives or the world's highest polluting nations is likely to be supplemented with a chart that allows the reader to make a quick size comparison without having to read the full text. Information presented in charts and tables is intended to send a message for our interpretation. To support this interpretation, an understanding of the different ways that data can be collected and displayed will help us locate the key features of a chart. This assists our ability to gauge the accuracy of the message.

In real life, we don't collect and represent data without a purpose. A health worker may need to complete a patient's temperature chart or record a child's height and weight on a percentile chart. Certain job roles will require the collection and analysis of data in order to identify patterns and trends in performance. For example, a sports manager will be required to collect and analyse data that can be used to develop a team's physical performance.

Similarly for your learners, it is important to provide a purpose for them to collect, organize, illustrate and analyse data. Situations should be relevant and meaningful to the learners and ideally either based within their vocational area or connected in some way to their lives and personal values.

Sometimes learners can spend a disproportionate amount of time collecting or presenting data, often focusing on drawing and colouring bar charts from given data. In typical work sheet or textbook exercises, the questions that require an interpretation of the data collected or drawn appear towards the end of the questions. Learners who spend too much time colouring bars or pie chart sections may not reach the more challenging questions that require them to analyse or interpret the data. Textbook questions are useful because they are carefully designed to include information that can be fairly simply presented to help learners develop their skills in handling data.

In general, learners find it more difficult to interpret charts and diagrams than draw them. Describing a chart or explaining a trend may involve learners in using quite specific vocabulary, so it is important to introduce and reinforce correct terminology consistently.

In the workplace, safety information is often presented pictorially. Safety information should be self-explanatory and employers should ensure that all employees understand the meaning of different signs. Fire extinguisher identification signs usually provide information in the form of a table. Being able to select which fire extinguisher to use on a particular fire will involve tracking along a row and down a column to identify the specific extinguisher. It is clearly important that this can be carried out accurately because using a water fire extinguisher on an electrical fire, for example, could cause harm to the user.

Embedding reminders

✔ Provide learners with the opportunity to extract information from different sources.
✔ Present learners with a variety of different charts to interpret.

> ✔ Encourage learners to discuss the main components and any trends.
> ✔ Encourage learners to use correct terminology when presenting their findings and drawing conclusions.

Extracting and using information

Extracting information is an important part of handling data. Information can be extracted from maps, diagrams, timetables, plans, brochures and health and safety information charts. In the real world, we extract information when we want to find something out, so it is important to consider how you can introduce learners to a situation or a question that will involve them in finding information that is meaningful and relevant to them.

Information from authentic sources will be the most meaningful and likely to engage learners. For example, current sports, trade and health and safety information is available on the Internet, in newspapers, sports club publications and specialist trade magazines. To help learners engage with the data, they should be encouraged to actively search for and extract the information themselves.

Examples of data sources

Learners on a sports science course can be encouraged to read and interpret sports league tables and match fixtures.

Learners on travel and tourism courses can extract information from holiday brochures, check departure and arrival times from train timetables, and find the average rainfall or hours of sunshine in a holiday resort.

A bricklayer will be expected to extract information from construction diagrams, including scale drawings from an architect. The drawings will show the different elevations of a building, including views from the front, rear, side and a bird's eye view from above. The measurements will be in metric form, which will provide learners with a useful and realistic review of the metric measurement system.

Learners on a childcare course can use packets or jars of baby food to extract information about nutritional content. Often this data is presented in percentage form, which provides a good opportunity to review and use percentages in a practical context. Learners can use the extracted information to draw tables and charts that compare costs per hundred grams or that illustrate the percentage of carbohydrate, protein and sugars in different products (see Figure 10.1).

Baby food	Protein (g)	Carbs (g)	Fat (g)	Fibre (g)	Sugar (g)	Salt (mg)
Brand A						
Brand B						
Brand C						

Figure 10.1 Comparison of nutritional content of baby foods

All learners should be encouraged to interpret and use the timetables for their courses. Some will be able to use their timetables alongside the handbooks from awarding bodies, to check course content and assessment requirements.

Extracting information from tables is likely to involve learners in working both horizontally and vertically. Some learners find this difficult, so encourage them to use a ruler, their finger or a piece of card to help track along a row and down a column.

Types of data

Data can consist of numbers or words that are collected for statistical purposes. Large amounts of data can be difficult to interpret without some additional translation. In data handling, this translation is part of the way we organize, represent and analyse the data to help it become useful and informative.

Learners are often required to select an appropriate way to represent different types of data. The type of data collected or given will determine the type of graph that is appropriate. Data can be described as qualitative or quantitative.

Qualitative data is non-numerical. Learners will collect this type of data if they want to compare different characteristics, such as car manufacturer, hair colour or type of disease. Questions 1 and 3 in the reflective task at the beginning of this chapter provide examples of qualitative data. It might also be referred to as categorical data.

Quantitative data has a numerical value. Quantitative data is data that can be counted or measured; in either case, the result is a quantity. There are two types of quantitative data. Data that can be *counted* is called 'discrete' – for example, the number of cars on a production line or the number of clients a hairdresser sees in one day. Data that is obtained by *measuring*, such as height, weight and temperature, is called 'continuous', as it is measured on a continuous scale. Examples of continuous data include the height of a tree or the time taken to run 100 metres.

Challenge 1

Decide whether the following examples of data are qualitative or quantitative. If they are quantitative, decide whether they are discrete or continuous:

a)   The number of dogs being treated at a veterinary surgery.
b)   The breeds of the dogs being treated.
c)   The weight of each dog.

Data that is collected by the learners themselves is called **primary data**. Data that has been collected by someone else is called **secondary data**.

Useful sources for finding current data include the Office of National Statistics (ONS), which provides national, regional and local statistics. The ONS collects and publishes statistics relating to the economy, the workforce and the population in general. It is a useful source for finding raw data for learners to organize and present. It also offers access to publications and bulletins that present information from a variety of different settings, including tourism, child safety and well-being, crime statistics and life expectancy rates.

The Health and Safety Executive (HSE) provides information about health and safety at work, as do different trade organizations.

Collecting data

It is important to think about the purpose of any data collection activity.

The handling of data often involves learners in collecting, organizing and representing data about themselves. This may be their height or shoe size, or their mode of transport to college. Importantly, it should not be anything that might cause embarrassment to any member of the group. Traffic surveys that gather data about the make or colour of vehicles passing the college are also typical.

You now need to consider whether your learners need the information they are gathering and what they will gain from the activity. Some learners will enjoy data collection activities where they are active and possibly out of the classroom. The follow-up work to display the information will further engage them in drawing and colouring pictograms and bar charts. Other learners will view gathering data for the sake of it to be somewhat irrelevant. Apart from practising the skills required, the activity is unlikely to generate any meaningful learning that requires learners to think more deeply about their vocational course. It is preferable to begin a data collection activity with a problem or scenario that is of interest to the learners. It is possible that learners *are* interested in the different means of transport to the college, particularly if there is a shortage of secure storage spaces and they want to campaign for more cycle sheds.

Embedding reminder

✔ Introduce a scenario that requires learners to collect information that is relevant to the vocational area or has an impact on college life.

Task 10.1

Consider the two scenarios below. Think about what the learners will need to do in order to gather the data they need:

a) Learners on a catering course are involved in designing the menus offered in the canteen. They need to find out whether the meals currently offered are meeting consumer demand and whether there are any menu preferences.

b) Learners on a public services course want to find out whether regional crime is increasing or decreasing.

The first scenario requires the learners to carry out a survey that enables them to find the information they need. This is an example of collecting *primary* data.

The second scenario is most likely to involve the learners in researching regional crime statistics that have been recorded by the police or government in recent years. This information is *secondary* data, as it uses data that has already been collected by somebody else.

When collecting data in a survey, it is important to ensure that the data is representative of the population. The population consists of all members of the group being studied. For example, in the first scenario for Task 10.1, the population refers to all the students and staff at the college. Often, the population is too large to collect data from all members, so a representative sample will need to be selected. In some circumstances, the whole population is used and this is then called a 'census'. Every 10 years the government carries out a National Census that requires every household to complete a questionnaire.

Designing a questionnaire for use in a survey

- Questions should be short, easy to understand and not ambiguous or double-barrelled.
- The majority of questions should be closed questions that can be summarized and then used for statistical purposes.

- Avoid the use of leading questions.
- Categories for responses should cover all possibilities.

Representing and displaying data

Information is presented in diagrams and charts to help make the original or raw data more accessible and visually appealing. Patterns and trends in information are more likely to be emphasized in a visual image than observed in the raw data.

Learners are often required to select an appropriate chart to represent their data. Different charts are used to represent discrete and continuous data and some chart types may be more suitable for qualitative than quantitative data. It is helpful for learners to explore different ways of representing the same data to help them determine which format most effectively illustrates their data.

Embedding reminder

✓ Provide an opportunity for learners to explore different ways of representing the same data.

Let us now look at some different types of charts and graphs and consider which are most suitable for our purpose and for the data that has been collected.

Bar chart

Bar charts are used to display qualitative data and discrete quantitative data. A bar chart can be horizontal or vertical and can be represented by a solid line or a block.

Multiple bar charts show more than one bar for each category. They are useful for comparing results within a category, for example between male and female, across different years or different locations.

Composite bar charts divide each bar to display different component parts to enable a comparison (see Figure 10.2). If too many components are included in a composite bar chart, the result can be confusing and useful comparative information may be lost.

Learners are usually more familiar with a vertical bar chart than a horizontal bar chart, so it can be helpful for them to see both types and consider why information might be presented in each particular way.

- *Gaps are left between the bars to show that the scale is not continuous.*
- *A composite or stacked bar chart is useful for showing different components.*

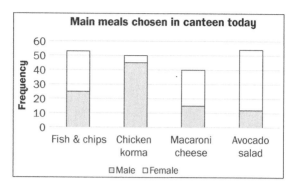

Figure 10.2 Bar chart to show main meal choices in college canteen by gender

Pictogram

Pictograms use pictures or symbols to represent quantities. They provide a simple representation of data and are often used in newspapers and magazines to provide a quick visual overview. Pictograms would not be suitable for identifying accurate statistical information in business documents.

A pictogram must have a key detailing the quantity each picture or symbol represents. When items are grouped, the picture or symbol needs to be carefully selected or designed. For example, learners on a motor vehicle course want to represent the numbers of cars of different manufacturers that a garage has in for repair each week. If a symbol of a car is chosen to represent 5 cars, it will be difficult to divide the icon to represent all possible quantities accurately.

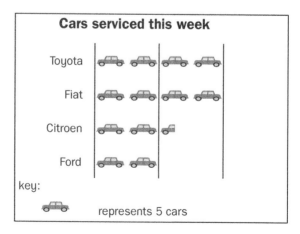

Figure 10.3 Pictogram showing the different types of car serviced in one week

- *Pictures for each category need to be the same size, to avoid misrepresenting the information.*

Pie chart

A pie chart is a good visual representation that shows the different parts that make up the whole. The area of the circle represents the whole and the area of each sector is proportional in size to the parts making the whole (see Figure 10.4). Pie charts are also good for showing the percentage that each part represents. They are most useful for qualitative data that is divided into a small number of categories.

Meals chosen in canteen today

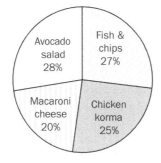

Figure 10.4 Pie chart to show total main meals served in college canteen

Constructing a pie chart from data will involve learners in using fractions and provides a helpful review of the number of degrees at the centre of a circle.

- *Carefully selecting the values will allow for differentiation within the task and so enable learners to construct either simple or more complex pie charts.*
- *More complex examples and those using data from real-life scenarios can be drawn using computer spreadsheet software.*

Line graph

A line graph is a useful way to show trends over a period of time. For example, a healthcare assistant may need to monitor and record a patient's temperature over a number of hours or days (see Figure 10.5).

In childcare, line graphs are often used to track changes in a child's weight or height. Children's weight and height measurements can be plotted on percentile charts to show a comparison with expected growth rates. In contrast,

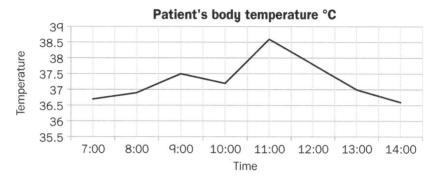

Figure 10.5 Line graph to show patient's temperature

a horticultural worker may wish to monitor and record the monthly growth of a new variety of fruit tree.

The horizontal or x-axis is used to represent time, which could be recorded in minutes, hours, days, months or years. The vertical y-axis records the measurement.

A line graph can be a useful way of comparing and analysing trends in different data sets that are plotted on the same diagram.

- *Line graphs are useful for displaying trends over time.*
- *Join the points with a straight line.*

Scatter graph

A scatter graph is useful when wanting to see if there is an association between two different things, or two variables. For example, height and shoe size are often linked – the taller someone is, the more likely they are to have longer feet and a larger shoe size.

In this case, one axis would be used to represent height and the other to represent shoe size. Points are plotted where the values for a person's shoe size meets their height. The resulting pattern of points can be analysed to determine whether there is a relationship between the two data sets. A narrow band of points can indicate a strong positive or negative correlation. Points that are widely scattered indicate that there is no correlation between the two sets of data.

A 'line of best fit' is a straight line drawn through the scatter points in such a way that the points are as evenly distributed about the line as possible. The closer the points are to the line, the stronger the correlation. The line of best fit can be used to make predictions about other values not included in the data set.

Showing that there is an association between two sets of data does not necessarily mean that one is the result of the other. Both variables might be influenced by another underlying cause.

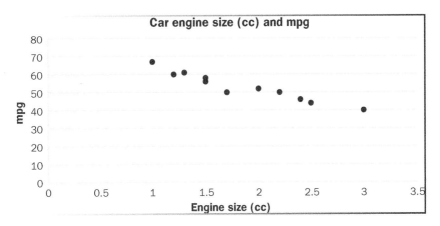

Figure 10.6 Scatter graph to show car engine size versus fuel economy

- *A positive correlation is when both variables increase or decrease together.*
- *A negative correlation is when one variable increases as the other decreases.*
- *No correlation indicates there is no obvious linear relationship between the data sets.*

Stem and leaf diagram

A stem and leaf diagram is a useful way to organize and display raw data. All the data values are shown in the diagram. The pattern of the leaves forms the same 'shape' as a horizontal bar chart.

A back-to-back stem and leaf diagram can be used to compare two data sets on one diagram.

A learner on a travel and tourism course, for example, could use a back-to-back stem and leaf diagram to display and compare spring temperatures in Colorado and New York (see Figure 10.7).

- *A stem and leaf diagram should always have a key.*

Colorado	Stem	New York
333377888	0	003333444446667778888899
11122222333444566666777788888999	1	1122245777899
011112222344	2	11223466778899
	3	0023
Key: 2|4 represents 24		

Figure 10.7 Back-to-back stem and leaf plot showing midday temperatures in Colorado and New York

Histogram

Histograms are used to represent continuous data, such as time, length or weight. Some histograms look like bar charts without the gaps between the bars. Other histograms have an unequal bar width. Large quantities of data can be grouped together in classes to reduce the number of categories and this may result in unequal column widths.

In a histogram, the area of each bar represents the frequency. The vertical axis is labelled frequency density, rather than frequency (see Figure 10.8). The frequency density is found by dividing the frequency of the class interval by the width of the class interval.

- *There are no gaps between the bars because a histogram displays continuous data.*
- *Sometimes column widths may be unequal.*

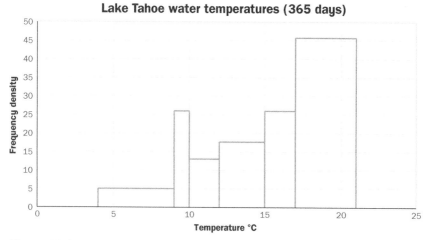

Lake Tahoe water temperatures (365 days)

Figure 10.8 Histogram showing surface water temperatures for Lake Tahoe

Box and whisker plot

A box and whisker plot, or a boxplot, is a useful way of displaying information about the spread of data and the median. It is useful for comparing different distributions on the same diagram.

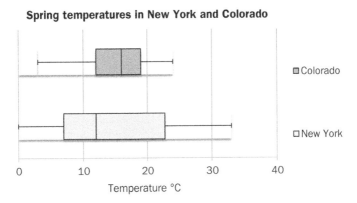

Figure 10.9 Box and whisker plot showing spring temperatures in New York and Colorado

The data used to generate the boxplot in Figure 10.9 is the same as the data used for the stem and leaf diagram in Figure 10.7. The end of each whisker on the boxplot shows the highest and lowest temperature for each location. The vertical line in each grey box is the median temperature. A boxplot also uses the lower and upper quartiles. When the data is placed in size order, the lower quartile is midway between the lowest value and the median, and the upper quartile is midway between the highest value and the median.

Look back at the median and the maximum and minimum temperatures in the stem and leaf diagram and locate each value in the corresponding box plot.

Using ICT to present data

Some of the charts presented as examples in this chapter have been drawn using Excel or other computer software packages. Many learners will be familiar with using Excel to create charts and graphs and they are often keen to find unusual charts for presenting their work. This creativity is good, although they may need reminders to check that the chart they have selected is appropriate and clearly illustrates the message portrayed by their data.

Analysing data

Finding the average and range

In everyday usage, most people have an understanding of what the word average means. In maths usage, there are different types of average which, when calculated, will provide a different average outcome for a given set of data.

> **Embedding idea**
>
> Write the word 'average' in the centre of a piece of paper, or for a small group activity in the centre of a piece of flip chart paper. Ask learners to record examples of where the word is used in everyday life and to create links to situations at work, home and in sport.

We may refer to average rainfall, average temperature, an average salary or an average score. The term average refers to a typical value that is representative of a set of data. When we have one typical value that represents a set of data, we are able to compare this value with another single measurement, or another typical value from a different data set.

The three common types of average are the mean, median and mode. It is important for learners to have an understanding of why they might need to calculate an average, and to be able to select which of the three averages is most appropriate to use in any given situation.

The **mean** is the most commonly considered average. It is calculated by adding all the values together, then dividing by the number of values.

+ The mean is a good measure to use if the data are spread fairly evenly.
+ The mean uses all the values in a data set.
− It is not possible to find the mean of a set of qualitative data.
− Extreme values, or outliers, will distort the mean.

The **median** is the value that occurs in the middle of the data after it has been placed in size order. If the data set has an odd number of data values, the median will be the middle number. In contrast, if the data set has an even number of values, the median will be the midpoint of the two central values (or the mean of those two numbers).

+ The median is not influenced by extreme values, so is a good measure to use if there are exceptionally high or low values.
− There will not be a median for some sets of qualitative data, unless the data can be logically ordered.

The **mode** is the value that occurs most often. There may be two or even three modes in a set of data. If all the data values are different, there will not be a mode.

+ The mode is very easy to find.
+ The mode is not affected by any extreme values.
+ The mode is the most appropriate average to use with categorical data, such as type of food or make of car, when we want to find the most popular type.
− The mode may not exist.

For data that is grouped, the category containing the most values is referred to as the *modal* class. Learners are sometimes confused when they see the term modal and may not recognize that it is linked to the mode.

Learners are sometimes surprised if an average is not one of the numbers that appears in the data set, or if they get a fractional average from a set of whole numbers. Familiarity with the methods of finding different averages is the most helpful approach here, so that learners can begin to appreciate why certain results might occur.

The extent to which the mean and the median are representative of the data set depends on the spread of the data. The **range** is a simple measure of dispersion that tells us how spread out the data is, by subtracting the lowest value from the highest value.

Challenge 2

A small health club has 7 employees. The annual salary for each employee is as follows:

£12,750 £3,800 £17,200 £8,450 £12,750 £14,500 £68,000

1. Calculate the mean, median, mode and range of the salaries.
2. Justify why someone might choose to use the mean value to represent the average salary.
3. Which value would you use to represent the average salary?

Interpreting information

Data presented in charts and graphs should provide a clear message. Sometimes information is presented in such a way as to mislead the reader. This may be due to poor presentation or the wrong choice of graph, but we also need to consider whether the chart has been designed to create a false impression intentionally. When looking at any graph or chart, it is important to check some key features:

● Graphs and charts need to have a title that explains what the chart is intended to show.
● The axes are clearly labelled.
● The scale starts at zero or clearly shows a break in the axis.
● A key is presented where necessary.
● Three-dimensional charts can distort perspective and create ambiguity when comparing proportion or reading from a scale.
● A sensible sample size is used that is representative of the population.
● Pictogram icons should be uniform in size and not scaled to represent real-life size.

Let us consider the effect that changing the scale or presentation style can have on different charts. The size of the bars in the chart on the left-hand side of Figure 10.10 suggests a significant increase in domestic burglary over the two-year period. The same information is represented in the chart on the right, but with the vertical axis starting at zero. Now the increase looks much less significant.

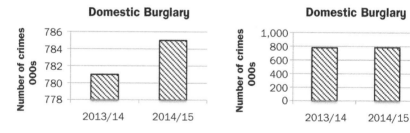

Figure 10.10 Misleading charts

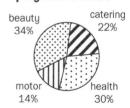

Figure 10.11 Changing the perspective

The three-dimensional pie chart shown on the left-hand side of Figure 10.11 can distort the appearance of the graph so that parts at the front are emphasized. Separating the sectors also makes comparisons difficult. The two-dimensional picture shows the size of each sector more clearly, even before the percentages are displayed.

Handling data terminology

As with the other topics considered here, data handling introduces its own particular vocabulary. New words need to be introduced, explained and reinforced regularly throughout a lesson to help familiarize learners with their meaning. Some of the words are specific to data handling and statistics, while others are familiar in everyday life, but have a specific mathematical meaning.

Some learners find it difficult to recall the precise meaning of the three words associated with average – the mean, median and mode. It can be helpful to think of the sounds of the words and to link the MOde with the MOst frequently occurring number. The median can be associated with the middle number, with an emphasis on the d, after the terms have been placed in numerical order. This just leaves the mean, which some learners say is the meanest one to calculate, as it requires the most work.

It is helpful to associate the range with an everyday term that uses the word. For example, if you think about the age range in a primary school, the children's ages range from 4 to 11, so the range of ages is $11 - 4 = 7$.

Looking at graphs provides a good opportunity to reinforce the x- and y-axes, while using the terms *plot along* and *plot up* can be used to reinforce the terms horizontal and vertical. Try to draw the terminology from the learners to see what they recall, rather than just feeding them the specific terms.

Learners may also confuse the direction of a row and a column. Encourage learners to hook each word to something they already know: boats are rowed across water; in architecture columns are upright.

Reflective task – suggestions

Question 1: Did you vote in the last election? Do you teach in a further education college?
Question 2: How old are you? What is your sleeve length in centimetres?
Question 3: What colour is your car? What is your favourite colour?

Challenge 1 – answers

a) Number of dogs treated – quantitative, discrete
b) Breed of dogs – qualitative
c) Weight of dog – quantitative, continuous

Challenge 2 – answers

Question 1

Mean: $\dfrac{3,800 + 8,450 + 12,750 + 12,750 + 14,500 + 17,200 + 68,000}{7} = \dfrac{137,450}{7} = £19,635.71$

Median: £3,800   £8,450   £12,750   **£12,750**   £14,500   £17,200
£68,000

Mode: £12,750 occurs twice

Range: £68,000 − £3,800 = £64,200

Question 2

The mean salary £19,635.71 could be used in marketing to represent the average salary if the company wanted to suggest that their employees were well paid. However, only one of the seven salaries is above the mean value. Here, the highest salary is an outlier that affects the mean average.

Question 3

The one high salary does not influence the median value and so this shows a more realistic average salary for the employees at the health club.

Further reading

FSSP (2008) *Teaching and Learning Functional Mathematics*. Available at https://www.ncetm.org.uk/public/files/578526/Functional+Maths+FINAL.pdf.

Griffiths, G. and Stone, R. (eds) (2013) *Teaching Adult Numeracy: Principles and Practice*. Maidenhead: Open University Press.

Griffiths, G., Ashton, J. and Creese, B. (2015) *Training to Teach Adults Mathematics*. Leicester: NIACE.

Index